CARE TO LOOK AT A DINNER MENU?

APPETIZER

~~~ Spinach Soup ~~~

ENTREE

Cassoulet

SALAD

Mixed Green Salad
with
Sour Cream French Dressing

DESSERT

Lemon Syllabub

And these are just a *few* of the dozens of fast, fantastic dishes you can whirl into gourmet meals for all occasions with THE NO TIME TO COOK BOOK. It's a "How To Succeed in the Kitchen without Really Cooking" guide that no modern woman will want to be without. In fact, it makes *eating in* as easy and enjoyable as *dining out!*

Other SIGNET Titles You Will Enjoy

THE
NO TIME
TO
COOK BOOK

Roslyn Beilly

A SIGNET BOOK from
NEW AMERICAN LIBRARY
TIMES MIRROR

SIGNET, SIGNET CLASSICS, MENTOR, PLUME AND MERIDIAN BOOKS
are published by The New American Library, Inc.,
1301 Avenue of the Americas, New York, New York 10019

FIRST PRINTING, OCTOBER, 1969

5 6 7 8 9 10 11 12 13

PRINTED IN THE UNITED STATES OF AMERICA

To Clyde, for one

CONTENTS

INTRODUCTION   9
    Suggested Aids to Quick Cookery   14
    Basic Information   15

1. OPENERS   23
    Dips   26
    Appetizers   31

2. SOUPS   43

3. FISH AND SHELLFISH   57

4. POULTRY   73

5. MEAT   85

6. COOPERATIVE COOKERY   103
    The Charcoal Grill   106
    The Fondue   111

7. SALADS AND SALAD DRESSINGS   115

8. SAUCES   139

9. VEGETABLES   151

10. RICE   171

11. QUICK DESSERTS   183
    Frozen Desserts   196
    Dessert Sauces   202

12. IRRESISTIBLE FOOTNOTES   205
    One Miracle Cake and Two Cookies   207
    Instant Breads   212
    Special Sandwiches   216
    Cheese Dishes   219
    Relishes   225

INDEX   229

INTRODUCTION

How To Succeed In The Kitchen Without Really Cooking—is the theme of this book. To turn out good, high quality meals with variety and imagination, without spending hours in the kitchen, may seem impossible, but it can be done.

Short-order cooking is not simply a matter of opening a few cans at seven minutes to six, however. It requires organization and advance planning. For one thing, you will need a well-stocked larder. Your supermarket is a treasure trove of jet-age convenience foods and cooking shortcuts—from frozen chopped onions to pre-melted chocolate. You can even buy disposable pots and pans—and you should.

Another factor in quick cooking is good equipment. Many of the recipes in this book are made in the electric blender, and I have assumed that you own one. Of course, you could use a sieve or a food mill instead, but those are horse-and-buggy methods in a streamlined age. I have listed on page 14 other gadgets and appliances which save time and work; check them against your own equipment and see what you need for this particular sleight-of-hand. Last-minute cooking requires up-to-date tools.

Here are a few of my shortcuts in the kitchen, some of which may suit your needs.

Any convenience food that saves time without sacrificing quality is fine. Frozen chopped onions are a good example. They taste just as good as fresh ones in cooked foods, and they eliminate all the time and tears of peeling, cutting, and chopping. But I find they cannot be used raw, because once thawed they are absolutely limp. So when it comes to salads and other foods where crispness counts, I chop my own.

There are one or two brands of condensed chicken broth on the market that are so good that I wouldn't dream of making my own stock. I use the broth just as it comes from the can—without diluting it—and keep what's left in a jar in the refrigerator. I use it for a variety of things—soup, sauces, gravies, and pot roasts. There are also canned gravies and sauces available that taste good with a bit of doctoring. You'll find them appearing in this book.

On the other hand, I prefer the taste of fresh lemon juice to any synthetic variety, and since I feel strongly about it, I squeeze my own. I also like freshly grated Parmesan cheese, and with a Mouli grater (an indispensable bit of equipment), it's no trouble to prepare. There is always a wedge of Parmesan in my refrigerator (it keeps and keeps), and when I need some, I grate it into a square of aluminum foil. Any leftover grated cheese is stored in a jar with a sprinkle top.

This brings me to another point. I love jars and use them constantly for making salad dressings and many sauces. My husband uses jars for mixing drinks to be stored in the refrigerator until serving time. I store soup and stock and cheese and raisins and nuts in jars. I use them to hold the contents of opened cans; I brandy peaches and pickle olives and marinate mushrooms in jars. They are convenient because you can see at a glance what's in them, you can close them tight for shaking or storing, and throw them away when you've used them without feeling wasteful.

Another indispensable item is plastic bags. What did we ever do without them? I use them for salad greens (which are washed, dried, torn, and ready to be tossed), for cut vegetables (with ice cubes for crisping), to keep bread and rolls fresh, for making cooky and cracker crumbs, and for storing extra ice cubes for a party. Plastic wrap is good for covering and storing foods, and aluminum foil is another handy aid in the kitchen. I use it for sifting flour, grating bread crumbs and cheese, mixing sugar and cinnamon or any dry ingredients. It's perfect for heating garlic bread, or covering food in the oven that's browning too fast. I use it, too, for making composed butter—butter mixed with anchovy paste, garlic, or herbs. The butter softens on a large square of foil, the other ingredients are blended into it, and the whole thing wrapped into a roll. After the roll is thoroughly chilled, I unwrap and cut it into even round slices which are pretty and easy to serve.

Cook-and-serve pots and pans are a boon to the busy cook. The cheapest and most practical of these are still the Pyrex oven-proof dishes which are brought to the table in wicker holders. But there are many attractive and useful brands on the market in ironstone, enamel, and earthenware. My favorite is a Greek taverna pot in copper with brass handles which looks beautiful at the table and somehow makes everything cooked in it taste superb.

Disposable cookware is the hurried cook's

best friend. The supermarkets are stocked with foil pans in all sizes and shapes—pie plates, baking and roasting tins, broiling pans with built-in racks—and I use them whenever I can. What a treat it is to broil a delicious steak and then throw away the pan!

Another must for quick cookery is advance preparation. The more you can do ahead, the easier the job at meal time. The great advantage of molded salads and desserts is that they can be made even a day ahead. Toss them together in the morning (or the day before), cover securely with plastic wrap, tuck them away in the refrigerator, and forget about them until serving time. In the same way, salad greens can be prepared ahead of time and stored in a plastic bag, ingredients for a casserole can be combined and refrigerated, vegetables can be marinated in dressing, a sauce can be made ahead and stored.

A glance at the recipes in this book will indicate that I am a herb enthusiast. In my opinion, herbs should be part of every cook's arsenal, and when you are striving for a gourmet dish in a hurry, herbs are absolutely essential.

In my New York apartment I have a small herb garden on my kitchen windowsill. Some of the plants, like parsley, chives, mint, and dill, come from a small market in my neighborhood. Others, like sage, tarragon, basil, and marjoram, I order by mail. Herbs are easy to grow, pretty to look at, and marvelously effective to snip and use in cooking.

More and more supermarkets are carrying fresh herbs these days. These will keep for a week or two in your refrigerator if you store them properly. Do not wash them, but pick off any dried or yellow leaves and pack them loosely in a small plastic bag sealed tight with a rubber band or plastic wire. Or store the herbs separately and loosely in small jars with screw-top lids.

Of course you can use dried herbs, but they lack the flavor of the fresh ones and are really not as effective.

A word about seasoning. Every recipe in this book is seasoned to my taste. Once you've tried them, you may want to subtract or add from the amounts given (the same is true of the amounts of wine given here), but to begin with you will at least have a clue about how much to use. Incidentally, I always use coarse salt and freshly ground black pepper when these are called for.

I think you will find that this book lives up to its promise of minimal preparation time. Occasionally, you will have to heat something, sauté it briefly, or pop it in the oven for a short time, but every one of the recipes is tailored to quick and easy production. In the interest of speed and simplicity, obviously there are many wonderful dishes that could not be included in this book. For instance, a good goulash, pot roast, or Chicken Kiev can't be whipped up in a few minutes. However, there are many others just as good which can.

Bonne chance and *bon appétit!*

SUGGESTED AIDS TO
QUICK COOKERY

Electric Blender
Portable Electric Beater
Toaster Oven
Mouli Grater
Wire Whisk
Garlic Press
Kitchen Scissors
Food Tongs
Vegetable Parer
Slotted Spoon
Rubber Spatula
Aluminum Foil
Disposable Cookware
Plastic Wrap (Rolls and Bags)
Assortment of Jars and Screw Tops
Cutting Board
Cooking Knives with Carbon Blades
(Paring, Chopping, Slicing)
Knife Sharpener
Fondue Set (Pot, Burner, and Long-Handled
Forks)
Charcoal Grill

Basic Information

SUBSTITUTIONS

1 square chocolate: 2½ T. cocoa and ½ T. shortening

1 C. pastry flour: 1 C. bread flour less 2 T.

1 t. baking powder: ¼ t. baking soda and ½ t. cream of tartar

1 C. milk:
   ½ C. evaporated milk and ½ C. water
   ½ C. condensed milk and ½ C. water (reduce sugar in recipe)

1 C. sour milk: 1 C. milk and 1 T. lemon juice or vinegar

1 C. butter or margarine: ⅞ C. salad or vegetable oil (recipe may need added salt)

1 C. sugar:
   ¼ C. corn syrup
   1 C. maple syrup (reduce liquid in recipe ¼ C.)
   1 C. honey (reduce liquid in recipe ¼ C.)
   1 C. molasses (add ¼ to ½ t. baking soda)

COMMON MEASUREMENTS

3 t. = 1 T.	12 T. = ¾ C.
4 T. = ¼ C.	16 T. = 1 C.
5⅓ T. = ⅓ C.	2 T. = 1 liquid oz.
8 T. = ½ C.	½ C. = 1 gill
10⅔ T. = ⅔ C.	

15

2 C. = 1 pt.   8 liquid oz. = 1 C.
4 C. = 1 qt.   1½ liquid oz. = 1 jigger
8 qts. = 1 peck   (there are also 1-oz.
4 pecks = 1 bushel   and 2-oz. jiggers)
1 liquid oz. = 2 T.

Butter:
  ½ lb. = 1 C.
  ¼ lb. = ½ C. (8 T.)
Flour (white): 1 lb. = 4 C.
Sugar
  (white): 1 C. weighs 7 oz.
  (brown): 1 C. (firmly packed) weighs 7 oz.
  (confectioners'): 1 C. weighs 4 oz.
Meat (chopped): ½ lb. = 1 C. (solidly packed)
Eggs (large):
  ½ whole egg = about 2 T.
  5 whole eggs = 1 C.
  8 to 9 whites = 1 C.
  12 yolks = 1 C.
Milk
  (evaporated): 1 14½ oz. can = 1⅔ C.
  (dry skim): 1 C. weighs 2⅓ oz.
    ¾ to 1 C. plus 4 C. of water make about 1
    qt. skim milk
Cornmeal: 1 C. weighs 5 oz.
Macaroni: 1 C. (4 oz.) measures 2¼ C. cooked
Noodles: 1 C. (2⅔ oz.) measures 1½ C. cooked
Oats (rolled): 1 C. weights 3 oz.
Rice: 1 C. (7 oz.) measures 4 C. cooked
Spaghetti: 1 C. (3⅓ oz.) measures 2⅛ C. cooked

OVEN TEMPERATURES

Very slow	250°F.	120°C.
Slow	300 F.	150 C.
Moderately slow	325 F.	165 C.
Moderate	350 F.	180 C.
Moderately hot	375 F.	190 C.
Hot	400 F.	205 C.
Very hot	450–500 F.	230–260 C.
Broiling	500 F. (or over)	260 C.

DEEP-FAT FRYING TEMPERATURES

Fritters, doughnuts, and uncooked mixtures	370°F.	190°C.
Croquettes, meatballs, or cooked mixtures	390 F.	200 C.
French-fried potatoes		
First frying	370 F.	190 C.
Second frying	390 F.	200 C.
Breaded chops	360–385 F.	180–195 C.
Fillets of fish	370 F.	190 C.
Small fish cooked whole	370 F.	190 C.

COOKING MEATS WITHOUT MEAT THERMOMETER

Cuts of meat	Temperature		Minutes per Pound
	300°F.	150°C.	
Best cuts of beef with bone (as standing rib roast)			rare 18–20
			medium 22–25
			well-done 35–40
	300 F.	150 C.	
Tender beef roasts without bone (as sirloin tip, rump roast, etc.)			rare 23–25
			medium 27–30
			well-done 40–45
Less tender cuts (chuck, etc.)	300–350 F.	150–180 C.	45
Lamb, pork, veal			
Ham	300–325 F.	150–160 C.	30–45
Chicken	300–325 F.	150–160 C.	30
Turkey	300–350 F.	150–180 C.	30
Braised meats	300–350 F.	150–180 C.	18–25
(browned first, then liquid added—use for very tough meats)	325–350 F.	160–180 C.	18–25

COOKING MEATS WITH MEAT
THERMOMETER

To use a meat thermometer, make an incision in the center of the meat through the fat side, and insert thermometer to center. Do not allow thermometer to rest on bone. Use oven temperatures given above.

Rare beef roast	140°F.	60°C.
Medium beef roast	160 F.	70 C.
Well-done beef roast	180 F.	80 C.
Medium or slightly rare lamb	170 F.	75 C.
Well-done lamb or mutton	180 F.	80 C.
Well-done veal	165 F.	73 C.
Well-done pork	185 F.	85 C.

APPROXIMATE CAN SIZES

Can Size	Weight	Contents
6 oz.	6 oz.	¾ C.
8 oz.	8 oz.	1 C.
#1	11 oz.	1⅓ C.
12 oz.	12 oz.	1½ C.
#303	16 oz.	2 C.
#2	20 oz.	2½ C.
#2½	28 oz.	3½ C.
#3	33 oz.	4 C.
#10	106 oz.	13 C

CONVERSION TABLE FOR
EQUIVALENTS

DRY INGREDIENTS

NOTE: To convert grams to oz., multiply grams
by 0.035
To convert oz. to grams, multiply oz. by
28.35

American and British (oz. and lbs.)	*Continental* (grams and kilograms)
.035 oz.	1 gram
½ oz. (1 T. or 3 t.)	14.18 grams
1 oz. (2 T.)	28.35 grams
3½ oz.	100 grams
4 oz. (approx.) or ½ C.	114 grams
8 oz. or 1 C.	226.78 grams
1 lb. or 2 C.	0.454 kilograms
2.21 lbs.	1 kilogram

LIQUID INGREDIENTS

NOTE: To convert liters to U.S. qts., multiply
the liters by 1.057.
To convert liters to British qts., multiply
the liters by 0.88.
To convert British qts. to liters, multiply
the qts. by 1.14.
To convert British qts. to U.S. qts.,
multiply the British qts. by 1.25.
To convert U.S. qts. to liters, multiply
the qts. by 0.95.
To convert U.S. qts. to British qts.,
multiply the U.S. qts. by 0.80.

Fluid Oz.	American	British (Imperial)	Continental
½	1 T. = 3 t.	½ T.	
1	2 T. = 6 t. = ⅛ C.	1 T.	
3½	6 T. plus 2 t.		
5	½ C. plus 2 T.	1 gill = ¼ pt. = ½ C.	
8	1 C. = ½ pt. = 16 T.	⅖ pt.	2.27 decilitres
10	1¼ C.	1 C. = 2 gills = ½ pt.	5.5 decilitres
			4.5 decilitres
16	1 pt. = 2 C. = ½ qt.		
20	1 pt. plus ½ C. = 2½ C.	1 pt. = 2 C. = 4 gills	
32	1 qt. = 2 pts. = 4 C.	⅘ qt.	
35	1 qt. plus ¼ C.	1¾ pts. = ⅞ qt.	1 litre
40	1 qt. plus ½ pt.	1 qt. = 2 pts.	
128	1 gal. = 4 qts. = 16 C.	3.2 qts.	3.785 litres

OPENERS

Hors d'oeuvres range from the simplest dip to the most complicated hot puffs, and they come from every corner of the world. They don't need to be elaborate to be good. One of my favorites is good black caviar which requires no fixing—only money. Serve it on a bed of cracked ice with paper-thin buttered pumpernickel, accompanied by lemon wedges, sour cream, and chopped onion. Another favorite is smoked salmon, sliced as thin as possible, arranged on buttered rye rounds and drizzled with oil, lemon juice, and capers. Freshly shucked clams with a sharp cocktail sauce are perfect hors d'oeuvres.

Here are some additional suggestions that are less of a strain on the budget. They seem to divide themselves into two categories—dips and appetizers.

DIPS

Dips are the easiest hors d'oeuvres, and, frankly, most of them are rather pedestrian. We have all had sour-cream-and-onion-soup up to here, and you'll find none of that ilk in this collection. Aside from the foreign dips like Guacamole, which is traditionally served with corn chips, and Hummus, which calls for flat round Iranian bread, I serve dips only as a foil for *crudités*.

Crudités (the French name for raw vegetables) can really dress up a simple dip. In addition to the usual vegetables like celery, carrots, and cucumbers, I serve a number of others. Raw cauliflowerets, white and red radishes, tender string beans, fresh white mushroom caps, thin green pepper strips, broccoli buds, scallions, even young asparagus tips make crunchy and delicious *crudités,* and can all be prepared in advance. I also include black or green olives and cherry tomatoes for color and taste.

When I have the time, I fill a large shallow bowl with crushed ice. In the center I set a small bowl piled high with anchovy or one of the sharper dips given in this section. Around the small bowl I arrange the cut raw vegetables like a bouquet.

When I'm in a hurry, I pile the vegetables, scrubbed and peeled but uncut, into a pretty wicker basket. I serve this with several small sharp knives so my guests can cut their own *crudités*. And when I'm in a big hurry, I substitute Russian or French dressing for a dip. When the variety of vegetables is unusual, an uncomplicated dip, if it is well-seasoned, will do.

ANCHOVY DIP

½ cup sour cream
½ cup mayonnaise
1 can (2 ounces) flat fillets of anchovy
1 clove garlic, crushed
1 tablespoon minced chives
Dash of seasoned salt
Freshly ground pepper

In a small bowl mix the sour cream and mayonnaise. Drain the anchovies, and cut them with a sharp knife into tiny pieces. (Chop them if it's easier, but it's really not necessary.) Add to mixture with crushed garlic, minced chives, salt, and pepper. Serve with crisp raw vegetables. Makes 1 cup.

SPICY AVOCADO DIP

1 avocado
1 package (3 ounces) cream cheese
2 tablespoons diced sweet roasted peppers
2 tablespoons mayonnaise
1 tablespoon lemon juice
1 tablespoon crumbled blue cheese
1 teaspoon horseradish
1 teaspoon coarse salt
4 turns freshly ground pepper
¼ teaspoon dry mustard

Peel and seed avocado. Cut into chunks and mash at high speed in blender with cream cheese. Add remaining ingredients and mix until blended. Serve with crisp crackers. Makes 1 cup.

BLACK BEAN DIP

1 can (10½ ounces) condensed black bean soup	Freshly ground black pepper
¼ cup sour cream	½ teaspoon Worcestershire sauce
1 clove garlic, crushed	3 drops Tabasco sauce
½ teaspoon coarse salt	1 tablespoon sherry

Turn all ingredients into a small bowl and mix until smooth. Chill. Serve with corn chips or raw vegetables. Makes about 1 cup.

GREEN CHEESE DIP

1 package (8 ounces) whipped cream cheese	¼ cup sour cream
	1 cup finely minced scallion greens
	¼ teaspoon salt

Mix cream cheese and sour cream until smooth. Add scallion greens and salt. Serve mounded with crackers or raw vegetables. Makes 1½ cups.

NOTE: You can add or substitute chopped chives, parsley, minced red radishes, chopped unpeeled cucumbers, or snipped fresh tarragon to this versatile dip. You can also make it spicier (if you like it that way) with Worcester-shire, Tabasco, or horseradish.

QUICK DIP

1 cup cream-style cottage cheese	1 clove garlic, crushed
2 tablespoons crumbled Roquefort cheese	¼ teaspoon coarse salt
	¼ teaspoon Worcestershire sauce
	Dash of paprika

In a small bowl combine the cottage cheese, Roquefort, garlic, salt, and Worcestershire. Chill until serving time. If the dip gets too stiff, add a drop or two of heavy cream. Mound the dip into a hollowed-out green pepper and top with a dash of paprika for color. Serve with raw vegetables. Makes 1 cup.

RED CAVIAR DIP

1 jar (2 ounces) red caviar	1 tablespoon mayonnaise
2 tablespoons sour cream	1 tablespoon chopped chives

Mix ingredients and chill. Serve with crisp crackers, black bread, or raw vegetables. Makes ½ cup.

WENDY'S HUMMUS

My niece brought this recipe back from a trip to Israel. It was completely new to me, but now that I am familiar with it, I notice the name on Lebanese and Armenian menus. Sometimes it is made with yogurt, but always with ground chick peas and tahin.*

1 can (20 ounces) chick peas, drained	1½ teaspoons coarse salt
1 clove garlic	Freshly ground pepper
3 tablespoons olive oil	1 tablespoon tahin
3 tablespoons lemon juice	Chopped parsley

Combine all ingredients except parsley at high speed in blender. Garnish with parsley and serve with flat Syrian bread cut in wedges. Makes 2 cups.

*Tahin is sesame seed paste used in halvah and other Near Eastern dishes. It can be found in special food shops. If you can't find it, leave it out. The hummus is almost as good without it, and so different from most hors d'oeuvres that it's worth a trial.

MARGE'S LIPTAUER

Marge's husband is Viennese, and this recipe is his mother's. There is nothing else to say about it, except that it's perfect!

1 cup (½ lb.) soft
  butter
1 package (8 ounces)
  cream cheese
1 can (2 ounces)
  anchovy fillets
1 tablespoon chopped
  chives

1 tablespoon capers
2 teaspoons dry mustard
2 teaspoons caraway
  seeds
½ teaspoon paprika
  Chopped parsley

Combine all ingredients except parsley at high speed in blender. Mound on a platter, sprinkle with chopped parsley, and serve with black bread, crackers, or crisp raw vegetables. Makes 2 cups.

APPETIZERS

Any of the following six recipes can be served separately as a first course or together in an antipasto assortment. If served as an antipasto, arrange them on a Lazy Susan or in glass bowls on a tray, and serve with plates and forks.

ANCHOVIES WITH PEPPERS

1 jar (7½ ounces)
  sweet roasted peppers
1 can (2 ounces) anchovy fillets
¼ cup red onion rings,
  thinly sliced
2 tablespoons capers

2 tablespoons red
  wine vinegar
1 teaspoon chopped
  parsley
½ teaspoon oregano
  Freshly ground
  pepper

Arrange the sweet roasted peppers, cut in half, in a shallow dish. Top with the anchovy fillets, reserving the oil. Scatter the onion rings and the capers over all. In a small screw-top jar, combine the oil from the anchovies with the vinegar, parsley, and oregano. Shake until blended, then pour over and around the peppers. Grind the pepper over the top, cover, and marinate in the refrigerator for at least 1 hour (the longer the better). Serves 4 as a first course or more in an antipasto assortment.

SPICED BEANS

1 can (20 ounces) garbanzos (cooked chick peas)	4 turns freshly ground pepper
1 teaspoon coarse salt	1 clove garlic, crushed
	½ teaspoon chopped parsley

Drain liquid from chick peas and rinse in cold water. Discard any loose skin. Add salt, pepper, crushed garlic, and parsley; toss lightly until blended. Cover and chill. Serve in a shallow bowl or dish and eat like peanuts. If you have a three-section bowl, serve with green olives and salted almonds.

NOTE: To serve as salad, heap beans on Boston lettuce leaves, drizzle some French dressing over the top, and garnish with slices of pimiento and anchovy fillets. Serves 4 as a first course or more in an antipasto assortment.

CANNELLINI WITH CAVIAR

1 can (20 ounces) cannellini (white kidney beans)
3 tablespoons olive oil

2 tablespoons lemon juice
2 tablespoons black caviar*
Freshly ground pepper

Drain cannellini and rinse thoroughly with cold water. Drain and marinate in olive oil and lemon juice one to two hours before serving time. Add caviar and pepper, toss lightly, and serve on lettuce leaf with lemon wedges. Serves 4-6 as a first course, more in an antipasto assortment.

*If black caviar is not available, or too expensive, the domestic variety can be used with great results; or mince a few scallions into the beans and add salt.

CECILY'S APPETIZER

Cecily was my first boss, and is still a dear friend. She is responsible for my interest in cooking, and for whatever standards of taste I have developed. She is a lady of vast knowledge and impeccable taste in food.

1 can (3¾ ounces) skinless and boneless sardines

1 can (4¾ ounces) caponata (egg plant appetizer)

Turn the sardines into a small shallow serving dish. Spoon the caponata over the sardines and mix lightly. Serve with hot buttered garlic bread or in an antipasto. Serves 4 as a first course, more in an antipasto.

MARINATED MUSHROOMS

2 cups button mushrooms	1 tablespoon coarse salt
1 cup tarragon or cider vinegar	1 clove garlic, split
½ cup finely minced onion	¼ teaspoon celery seed
2 tablespoons olive oil	¼ teaspoon sugar freshly ground pepper

Wash and dry mushrooms; do not peel or slice. Turn the mushrooms into a large screw-top jar. Add the remaining ingredients. Cover and shake lightly to combine. Refrigerate for at least 24 hours. Serve as an hors d'oeuvre with picks or as part of an antipasto tray. Serves 8.

PICKLED OLIVES

1 can (8 ounces) super colossal ripe olives	1 jar (7 ounces) sweet mixed pickles

Drain olives and turn into a large screw-top jar. Turn pickles and juice into blender, and liquefy at high speed for 1 minute. Add the liquified pickles and juice to the olives, cover, and refrigerate for 24 hours. Serve as an hors d'oeuvre, a relish, or in an antipasto.

CHEESE BALL I

2 cups grated mild cheese (like Gouda or Edam)
¼ teaspoon salt
1 clove garlic, crushed
1-2 tablespoons beer or ale*
¼ cup finely chopped parsley

Mix grated cheese with salt and crushed garlic. Add enough beer to make the mixture firm enough to mold into a ball. Roll ball in chopped parsley. Chill before serving. Serve with warm melba toast or assorted crackers. Serves 8.
*If you don't have any beer (or ale) on hand, use light or heavy cream.

CHEESE BALL II

1 package (3 ounces) cream cheese
1 package (3 ounces) blue cheese
½ cup grated cheddar cheese
1 tablespoon grated onion
½ teaspoon Worcestershire sauce
½ cup coarsely chopped peanuts

Place the three cheeses on a piece of aluminum foil and let stand in warm place until softened. Add onion and Worcestershire sauce and wrap up the foil. Shape into a ball and chill for 2-4 hours. A few minutes before serving, remove ball from foil, roll in nuts, and place on serving dish surrounded by thin, crisp crackers. Serves 8.

DONNA'S CRABMEAT TURNOVERS

My daughter invented these turnovers. The same dough can be used for cocktail frankfurters and tiny pizzas.

1 can turnover pastry dough*
1 can (7 ounces) crabmeat
2 tablespoons mayonnaise
¼ teaspoon garlic salt

Separate dough into 8 squares. Roll each square on a lightly floured surface until paper-thin. Cut into 4 squares; cut each square into 2 triangles. (You will have 8 triangles for each original square.)

Pick over crabmeat to remove any scales. Mix with mayonnaise and garlic salt. Place a dab of crabmeat in the center of each triangle. Fold each of the 3 points into the center and pinch. Heat until golden brown in a moderately hot oven—about 10 minutes. (You can heat these in your toaster oven.) Makes 64.

*Turnover pastry dough can be found in the dairy department of your supermarket as part of a package of ready-to-bake fruit turnovers.

Esther's Pate I and II

My sister-in-law, who is a great hostess, gave me both these pâté recipes. She always uses a brand called Mother Goose liverwurst, but any good brand will do. Both versions are excellent, and very pretty served with sprigs of parsley.

ESTHER'S PATE I

2 packages (6 ounces each) liverwurst	2 tablespoons mayonnaise
2 tablespoons grated onion	2 tablespoons bourbon or cognac

Mash liverwurst with a fork. Add onion, mayonnaise and bourbon or cognac; mix until blended. Pack into an oiled mold and chill until serving time. Makes 1½ cups.

ESTHER'S PATE II

1 tablespoon (1 envelope) unflavored gelatin	drained
	8 pitted ripe olives, sliced
1 can (10½ ounces) condensed beef consommé, piping hot	¾ pound liverwurst
	¼ cup sour cream
	2 tablespoons chopped parsley
2 cans (4 ounces each) chopped mushrooms,	½ teaspoon Worcestershire sauce

Into the blender put the gelatin, hot beef consommé, and mushrooms. Cover and blend on high speed for 30 seconds. Add olives, liverwurst, sour cream, parsley and Worcestershire sauce. Blend on high speed for 1 minute, or until thoroughly blended. Turn into a mold

which has been rinsed in cold water. Cover and
chill until firm. Turn out on small tray, garnish
with olive slices and parsley, and serve surrounded with crackers or thin rye rounds.
Serves 12.

GUACAMOLE

1 medium avocado	¼ teaspoon coarse
1 tablespoon lemon	salt
juice	¼ teaspoon Worcester-
2 teaspoons grated	shire sauce
onion	Freshly ground
	pepper

Peel and seed the avocado. Mash with a fork
into a paste. Add lemon juice, onion, salt,
Worcestershire, and about 4 turns of pepper.
Serve with corn chips. Makes 1 cup.

NOTE: There are endless ways to vary this Mex-
ican dip. You can add 2 crumbled cold bacon
slices, 2 tablespoons of chopped almonds or
cashew nuts, ½ can of anchovies, or extend it
with a 3-ounce package of cream cheese. Or
you can heighten the taste with a few drops of
Tabasco, a tablespoon of chili sauce, a tablespoon of sherry, or a dab of horseradish.

HERRING WITH APPLES

1 jar (12 ounces)
  herring in wine
  sauce
½ cup thinly sliced
  sweet onion
1 tart apple
¾ cup sour cream
¼ teaspoon sugar

Drain the juice from the herring, but don't discard it. Cut the tidbits in half if you are going to serve them as hors d'oeuvres. Add the sliced onion (red or white). Cut the apple into small cubes but don't peel it. Add to the herring with sour cream and sugar. If too thick, add 1 to 2 tablespoons of the reserved liquid. Cover and chill until serving time. Serve as first course on lettuce, or as an hors d'oeuvre with thinly sliced pumpernickel or crisp crackers. Serves 4 as a first course, more as an hors d'oeuvre.

MELON WITH PROSCIUTTO

1 honeydew melon
½ pound (about)
  prosciutto (Italian
  smoked ham)

Cut melon into cubes, or (if you have a melon-ball cutter) scoop out the melon. Wrap each cube or ball with a strip of prosciutto. Fasten with a toothpick. Chill and serve. Serves 4.

SCALLOP SEVICHE

It's hard to believe that this recipe works, but it does—superbly. The lime juice (which must be fresh) has enzymes which somehow "cook" the scallops. The flavor is delicate and different.

1 pound sea scallops	3 tablespoons olive oil
½ cup fresh lime juice	1 tablespoon white wine vinegar
2 tablespoons chopped onion	¼ teaspoon coarse salt
2 tablespoons chopped green pepper	Freshly ground pepper

Drain the scallops, rinse them in cold water, and cut them into quarters. Cover with lime juice and marinate in the refrigerator for 3 or 4 hours. The lime juice will change the color of the scallops from translucent to white. Drain the scallops, add remaining ingredients, and serve on a bed of lettuce. Serves 4 as a first course or more as an hors d'oeuvre with toothpicks.

SHRIMP IN MUSTARD SAUCE

¾ cup oil (1 part olive and 1 part salad)	1 hard-cooked egg
¼ cup wine vinegar	¼ cup diced celery
1 tablespoon Dijon mustard	¼ cup diced green pepper
½ teaspoon coarse salt	1 tablespoon grated onion
⅛ teaspoon sweet paprika	1 tablespoon minced parsley
	2 cups cooked shrimp

Combine oil, vinegar, mustard, salt, and paprika in the blender at low speed. Add egg, celery, green pepper, onion, and parsley; blend at low speed for 5 seconds. Pour over shrimp, cover, and chill until serving time. Serve with long picks and pilot biscuits. Serves 4-6.

SHRIMP TOLEDO

I tasted this at the luxurious Toledo Restaurant in New York, and improvised the recipe. It's an unusual appetizer, and equally good as a salad. The combination of shrimp and fruit is irresistible.

2 cups cooked shrimp
1 cup orange or grapefruit sections (fresh or jarred)
¼ cup mayonnaise
1 tablespoon chili sauce
1 tablespoon lemon juice
1 tablespoon minced fresh dill *or*
1 teaspoon dried dill weed
1 teaspoon coarse salt
¼ teaspoon Worcestershire sauce
Freshly ground pepper

In a medium bowl mix all ingredients carefully. Cover and chill until serving time. Serve on a bed of Boston lettuce. Serves 4 as a first course.

NICKY'S PATE

Nicky is my married stepdaughter, and an adventurous cook. She serves this pâté with cucumber slices and crisp sesame wafers.

1 cup leftover tongue
1 cup pitted ripe olives
1 tablespoon softened butter
2 tablespoons mayonnaise
1 teaspoon grated onion
⅛ teaspoon dried thyme

Chop or grind the tongue and olives thoroughly. Add softened butter, mayonnaise, onion, and thyme. Pack into a small mold which has been buttered or rinsed in cold water, cover, and chill. Turn out on a serving dish and serve with crisp crackers or thinly slices buttered rỳe bread. Makes 2 cups.

Soups

After a long eclipse, soup is coming back into favor. For one thing, the blender has eliminated the tedium of chopping, mashing, and sieving. For another, ready-to-serve soups are getting better all the time. While the makers of canned soup work for new and better products, dehydrated and frozen soups have been developed, and they are excellent.

Quick and easy soups fall into two main categories. One type uses cooked, canned, or leftover vegetables blended with liquid and seasoning. The other type starts with a prepared soup as a base, and improvises on it with extra ingredients. Sometimes just a tablespoon or two of sherry will transform an ordinary soup into a memorable one.

Whatever soup you serve, and the variety is endless, serve it with dash. I will always remember a meal I had at a friend's home when I was a girl. I realize now that what impressed me so much was just a can of tomato soup mixed with a can of pea soup, but it was served in paper-thin china cups with a dollop of salted whipped cream and some chopped peanuts. I felt as if I were at a royal banquet.

AVOCADO-CLAM BISQUE

1 ripe avocado, diced	1 tablespoon lemon
1 can (7 ounces)	juice
minced clams	1 teaspoon coarse salt
1 cup cream or milk	1 teaspoon Worcester-
1 cup chicken broth	shire sauce
	Dash cayenne

Combine all ingredients in blender. Blend at low speed for 1 minute. Chill thoroughly. Serve in chilled cups. Sprinkle with chopped chives or parsley. Serves 4-6.

QUICK BORSCHT

I've used this recipe for years. Served cold, it's a summer staple at our house, and helps to round out a quick salad supper.

1 can (8 ounces)	1 slice onion
beets with liquid	1 teaspoon coarse
1 cup chicken con-	salt
sommé	1 tablespoon sugar
½ cucumber, sliced	1 tablespoon chopped
¾ cup sour cream	chives
2 tablespoons lemon	½ teaspoon dill weed
juice	

Combine all ingredients in blender at low speed. Chill thoroughly. Serve in chilled cups with paper-thin lemon slices. Or, if you prefer hot borscht, heat, but do not boil. Serves 4-6.

MILLIE'S CABBAGE SOUP

The inventor of this soup says she never makes this soup the same way twice, but this is her basic recipe. Leftover chicken, ham, frankfurters, or tongue, added a few minutes before serving, will make it even heartier.

1 can (1 pound)
  sauerkraut
1 can (1 pound)
  peeled whole
  tomatoes

1 cup chicken broth
2 teaspoons sugar

In a medium saucepan combine the sauerkraut with liquid, the tomatoes with liquid, and the chicken broth. Heat slowly until flavors mingle and soup is piping hot. Add sugar, stir, and taste. Serve with crusty bread. Serves 6.

CREAM OF CARROT SOUP

1 can (10 ounces) frozen cream of potato soup
1 cup chicken broth

1 jar (4 ounces) puréed carrots*
2 tablespoons butter
2 tablespoons cream

Heat the soup according to directions, using chicken broth as liquid. Add carrots, butter, and cream. Serve garnished with minced parsley or chives. Serves 3-4.

*Puréed carrots can be found in the baby foods section of your supermarket.

CONSOMMÉ RUSSE

2 cans (12½ ounces   2 teaspoons lemon
   each) jellied con-   juice
   sommé   1 teaspoon coarse salt
¼ cup sour cream   1 jar (2 ounces) red
2 tablespoons sherry   caviar

Combine the consommé with sour cream,
sherry, lemon juice, and salt. Chill until jellied.
Serve in cold consommé cups; top each serving with a dollop of red caviar. Serves 6.

CREAMY VEGETABLE SOUP

1 can (10 ounces) fro-   1 cup leftover cooked
   zen cream of shrimp   vegetables*
   soup, thawed   2 tablespoons sherry
1 cup cream or milk

Into a medium saucepan stir the soup,
cream or milk, vegetables, and sherry. Heat to
the boiling point, season if necessary, and
serve. Serves 4.
*This can be any combination of leftovers—carrots,
peas, corn, broccoli, potatoes, or even cabbage. Salt
and pepper depends on the amount of seasoning in
the vegetables.

CRAB BISQUE

1 can (7 ounces)
   crabmeat
2 tablespoons sherry
1 can (10½ ounces)
   tomato soup

1 can (10½ ounces)
   green pea soup
1 cup light cream
½ teaspoon sweet
   paprika

Carefully pick over crabmeat. Add sherry and let stand. In a medium saucepan combine the soups with the cream and paprika. Heat, but do not boil. Add crabmeat and sherry, heat and serve immediately. Serves 6.

FROSTY CUCUMBER SOUP

2 cups buttermilk
1 large or 2 medium
   cucumbers, peeled
   and cubed
2 tablespoons chopped
   chives or green on-
   ions

2 tablespoons chopped
   parsley
2 teaspoons coarse salt
4 turns freshly ground
   black pepper

Combine all ingredients in blender at low speed. Or, if you prefer some texture, coarsely grate the cucumber and combine all the ingredients in a screw-top quart jar. Chill thoroughly. Serves 4-6.

ICED CURRY SOUP

1 can (10½ ounces) cream of chicken soup	1 tablespoon lemon juice
1 cup cream	½-1 teaspoon curry powder

Combine soup and cream in a bowl or blender. Measure lemon juice into a small cup. Add curry powder and mix into a paste. Add to soup and blend. Chill before serving. Serve in chilled cups with paper-thin lemon slices. Serves 2-3.

Gazpacho I and II

No soup glossary would be complete without a recipe for Gazpacho. The first recipe is a good easy one for a standard Spanish version. The second recipe is like no other Gazpacho I know, but it's so good I had to include it.

GAZPACHO I

4 tomatoes, cut in quarters	2 tablespoons olive oil
1 cucumber, sliced	2 tablespoons white wine vinegar
6 pitted ripe olives	1 tablespoon coarse salt
½ cup chopped onion	
½ cup chopped green pepper	1 teaspoon Worcestershire sauce
2 tablespoons chopped chives	Freshly ground pepper
2 cloves garlic, minced	

Combine all ingredients in blender at medium speed. Chill thoroughly. Serve in bowls surrounded by crushed ice or plunk an ice cube or two into every bowl. Serves 4-6.

GAZPACHO II

½ cup olive oil	Freshly ground
¼ cup white wine vinegar	pepper
1 egg	1 can (1 pound) peeled tomatoes
¼ cup blanched almonds	1 cucumber, partially peeled
2 cloves garlic, sliced	6 slices stale bread
1 teaspoon salt	1-2 cups chicken broth

Turn oil, vinegar, egg, almonds, garlic, salt, and pepper into blender. Blend at high speed for 90 seconds. With a rubber scraper, scrape this mixture into a medium bowl. Then turn the tomatoes with their liquid into the blender. Dice the cucumber and add. Cut the crusts from the bread, cut into cubes, and add. Blend for 60 seconds at low speed. Add to the mixture in the bowl and stir until blended. Add chicken broth until the mixture reaches the right consistency. Chill thoroughly. Serve with an ice cube in each bowl. Serves 6.

HOT LIMA BEAN SOUP

2 cans (10½ ounces each) chicken broth
1 cup chopped onion
2 cups cooked lima beans (1 pound can), drained

1 teaspoon coarse salt
¼ teaspoon caraway seed, crushed
1 clove garlic, crushed
2 knockwurst, sliced

In a medium saucepan, heat the chicken broth with onion, lima beans, salt, crushed caraway seed, crushed garlic, and sliced knockwurst until heated through and boiling hot. Serves 5-6.

ONION SOUP

I guess I love onion soup because it reminds me of Les Halles in Paris. At any rate, here is a quick recipe that manages to taste like the real thing—bread, cheese, and all.

1 can (10½ ounces) onion soup
1 cup chicken broth

8 thin slices French bread
1 cup freshly grated Parmesan cheese

Heat onion soup and chicken broth until boiling. Divide into 4 oven-proof ramekins. Float a slice of French bread on each. Sprinkle with 2 tablespoons of grated cheese. Top with another slice of bread and 2 more tablespoons of cheese. Heat in a very hot oven or under the broiler until the top is brown and melted. Serve with a spoon and fork and a tossed green salad. Serves 4.

CREAMY PUMPKIN SOUP

If anyone had predicted before I discovered this recipe that I would rave about pumpkin soup, I'd have said he was crazy. But this soup is marvelous, and you should try it...

2 tablespoons butter
½ cup chopped onion
½ cup chopped green pepper
1 tomato, peeled and chopped
1 tablespoon minced parsley
{ 1 teaspoon minced thyme *or*
¼ teaspoon dried thyme

1 can (1 pound) pumpkin
1 cup chicken broth
½ cup cream or milk
1 teaspoon coarse salt
¼ teaspoon sugar
¼ teaspoon ground nutmeg

In a medium saucepan melt the butter. Add onion, green pepper, tomato, parsley, and thyme and cook until soft. Add pumpkin and chicken broth and simmer for a few minutes. Add cream or milk, salt, sugar, and nutmeg. Heat until piping hot. Serves 6.

PUREE MONGOLE WITH CLAMS

1 can (10½ ounces) cream of tomato soup
1 can (10½ ounces) green pea soup
1 can (7 ounces) minced clams, drained

1 cup milk or light cream
¼ teaspoon Worcestershire sauce
Dash of Tabasco sauce, if desired

In a medium saucepan combine the soups, minced clams, milk or cream, Worcestershire sauce, and Tabasco (if you want to heighten the flavor). Heat until piping hot, but do not let boil. Serves 6.

TOMATO DILL SOUP

Dill is probably my favorite herb. Here it adds much to the flavor of the tomato. Use your kitchen scissors to mince the dill. If you serve this hot, be sure it doesn't boil or the sour cream will curdle and separate.

1 can (10½ ounces) tomato soup
1 tomato, peeled and chopped
½ cup sour cream

½ cup cream or milk
1 tablespoon minced fresh dill
½ clove garlic, crushed

Combine soup, tomato, sour cream, milk or cream, dill, and crushed garlic. Serve very hot

or very cold. Garnish with minced parsley.
Serves 3-4.

SHRIMP BISQUE

1 can (10 ounces)   1 teaspoon lemon
  frozen cream of   juice
  shrimp soup   ½ teaspoon coarse
1 cup cream or milk   salt
1 ripe avocado, diced   Dash of nutmeg
1-2 tablespoons sherry   1 can (4½ ounces)
                             cooked shrimp

In a medium saucepan, stir the soup, cream
or milk, avocado, sherry, lemon, salt and nutmeg. Heat until bubbling. Drain and rinse the
shrimp and add just before serving. Serves 4.
NOTE: This soup may be served cold. Sieve the
avocado, combine all the ingredients, and chill.
Serve in chilled cups, and top with chopped
chives or parsley.

SAVORY SPINACH SOUP

1 can (10 ounces)   1 cup cream
  frozen cream of po-   1 teaspoon coarse
  tato soup, thawed   salt
1 cup chicken broth   ¼ teaspoon dried
¼ cup chopped scal-   marjoram
  lions   Freshly ground
1 can (8 ounces)   black pepper
  chopped spinach,
  drained

Turn all ingredients into blender. Blend at low speed for 1 minute. Serve hot or cold. Serves 4-6.

VICHYSSOISE

Of course, this is not the classic vichyssoise which is made with leeks and chicken broth, but it does very well as a quick substitute for the real thing.

1 can (10 ounces)
    frozen cream of
    potato soup,
    thawed
½ cup cream
½ cup milk

2 tablespoons
    chopped chives
1 teaspoon coarse salt
    Freshly ground
    black pepper

Combine all ingredients in blender at low speed. Chill thoroughly. Serve in chilled cups and sprinkle with additional chopped chives, chopped parsley, or chervil. Serves 4-6.

Fish & Shellfish

Volumes have been written about fish cookery. For the cook who is looking for variety in her menus, a cookbook entirely devoted to fish is a good investment.

Let us consider here some of the aids to instant fish cookery. Canned fish and seafood immediately come to mind. Canned salmon and tuna fish have been American staples for years; sardines and anchovies can only be purchased in cans. Shellfish such as shrimp, crabmeat, lobster, oysters, even steamed clams come in cans, and all are excellent items for your pantry shelf.

Newer on the market, and closer to the taste of fresh fish, are the frozen varieties. Most of the shrimp dishes in this volume were tested with packaged frozen cooked shrimp, which are firm and have flavor; frozen shrimp are also available raw—cleaned and ready to cook. Fresh crabmeat and lobster meat are flash frozen in tins. Rock lobster is frozen and packaged in cartons. Frozen fish fillets and steaks are sold in the supermarket, and are certainly worth a try.

Of course the best fish is fresh fish, and here your closest ally is your fish dealer. He will tell you what fish is plentiful (and therefore cheap) and what cuts are most convenient. If he's like my fish dealer, he has great recipes to share. You'll find some quick ideas for cooking fresh fish fillets in the book—you'll improvise many others. Remember, too, that fish steaks (like swordfish, haddock, and striped bass) are really easy to prepare. Just arrange them in a disposable foil broiling pan, dot generously with butter, lemon juice, a sprinkling of dry vermouth, and paprika and broil until brown. Don't overcook them—the steaks should be moist. Nothing could be simpler—or more delicious!

CLAM BAKE

1 cup soda cracker crumbs	2 tablespoons chopped onion
1 cup milk	2 tablespoons chopped green pepper
2 eggs, slightly beaten	
1 can (7 ounces) minced clams	¼ teaspoon coarse salt
1 can (8 ounces) whole kernel corn, drained	½ teaspoon Worcestershire sauce
	¼ cup freshly grated Parmesan cheese

Mix cracker crumbs with milk and slightly beaten eggs. Let stand while you prepare the rest of the casserole. Turn the clams, with their liquid, the drained corn, onion, green pepper, salt, and Worcestershire sauce into a medium oven-proof casserole. Add crumb-milk-egg mixture. Sprinkle with Parmesan cheese. Heat in a moderate (350 degree) oven for about 40 minutes or until set. Serves 2-3.

BAKED CRABMEAT

This dish is delicious, but should be made only with frozen or, preferably, fresh crabmeat. I've tried it with canned crabmeat and it just doesn't work. There are dishes that taste good with canned crabmeat—this doesn't happen to be one of them.

½ pound (about 2 cups) lump crabmeat (fresh or frozen)

¼ cup cracker crumbs*

½ cup minced onion

½ cup cream or milk

1 tablespoon sherry

½ teaspoon coarse salt

½ teaspoon dry mustard

3 tablespoons butter

3 tablespoons freshly grated Parmesan cheese

Carefully mix crabmeat with crumbs, onion, cream or milk (or a mixture of the two), sherry, salt, and mustard. Turn into 3 individual buttered oven-proof ramekins. Dot each one with a tablespoon of butter, then a tablespoon of cheese. Heat in a hot (400 degree) oven for 10 minutes or until piping hot. Serves 3.

*Make your own cracker crumbs by crushing a few saltines in your fist. I've made this dish with rye crackers, sesame seed crackers, and butter wafers—it's always marvelous. Just adjust the salt when you use salty crackers.

CRABMEAT AU GRATIN

1 can (10 ounces) frozen cream of shrimp soup, thawed

½ cup sour cream

1 can (7 ounces) crabmeat

1 can (4 ounces) sliced mushrooms, drained

1-2 tablespoons sherry

1 tablespoon chopped chives

1 teaspoon grated onion

¼ teaspoon Worcestershire sauce

¼ teaspoon dry mustard

⅓ cup grated Parmesan cheese

Into a medium saucepan, turn the thawed soup and sour cream. Pick the scales out of the crabmeat and add with drained mushrooms, sherry, chives, onion, Worcestershire, mustard, and cheese. Heat thoroughly and serve on Holland Rusk, toasted English muffins, or toast. Serves 3-4.

NOTE: If you prefer to heat in the oven, leave out the grated Parmesan cheese. Pour into individual baking shells or ramekins, sprinkle the grated cheese over the top (adding more if you need it) and heat in hot oven until bubbling.

HOT CRABMEAT SALAD

2 cans (7 ounces each) crabmeat
1 tablespoon lime juice
2 packages (3 ounces each) cream cheese, softened
¼ cup mayonnaise
1 tablespoon grated onion
1 tablespoon chopped chives
2 teaspoons Worcestershire sauce
1 clove garlic, crushed
½ teaspoon salt
Dash of Tabasco sauce

Carefully pick over crabmeat. Add lime juice and let stand while you combine the remaining ingredients. Add crabmeat mixture and pile into 1 quart oven-proof casserole or 4 individual baking shells. Heat in a moderate (350 degree) oven until bubbling. Serves 4.

FILLETS IN CREAM SAUCE

1½ pounds fish fillets
2 tablespoons chopped onion
1 can (10½ ounces) cream of mushroom soup
2 tablespoons cream or milk
2 tablespoons white wine or lemon juice
Dash of paprika

Arrange the fish fillets in a buttered shallow oven-proof dish. Sprinkle with chopped onions. In a small bowl mix the soup, cream or milk, and wine or lemon juice until smooth. Pour over the fillets. Add a dash of paprika. Bake in a moderate (350 degree) oven for 20 minutes. Serves 4.

FILLETS IN SHRIMP SAUCE

1½ pounds fish fillets
2 tablespoons chopped scallions or shallots
1 can (10 ounces) frozen cream of shrimp soup, thawed
1 tablespoon lemon juice

Arrange the fish fillets in a buttered shallow oven-proof dish. Sprinkle with chopped scallions or shallots. Pour thawed cream of shrimp soup over the fish. Sprinkle with lemon juice. Bake in a moderate (350 degree) oven for 20 minutes. Serves 4.

OVEN-FRIED FILLETS

1 pound fish fillets
½ cup milk
1 teaspoon coarse salt
   Freshly ground
   black pepper

½ cup flavored bread
   crumbs
2 tablespoons butter

Heat oven to 500 degrees. Dip the fillets in milk which has been mixed with salt and pepper. Then dip the fillets into the flavored bread crumbs. You may need to add some additional bread crumbs. Place the fillets in a buttered flat baking dish (or two) so that they do not touch. Dot lightly with butter. Bake until they are crisp and gold-brown, about 12-15 minutes. Serve with parsley and lemon. Serves 3-4.

ESCABECHE OF FLOUNDER

2 pounds fillet of
   flounder
1 cup fresh lime juice
1 clove garlic
3 tablespoons lemon
   juice
6 tablespoons orange
   juice

⅓ cup olive oil
½ teaspoon salt
3 tablespoons
   chopped chives
   Few drops Tabasco
   sauce

Cut fish into tiny slivers and marinate in lime juice for at least 2 hours. In a medium mixing bowl, crush the garlic, add remaining ingredients, and blend. Add the fish, which has been drained; refrigerate for 24 hours. Garnish with ripe olives and serve. Serves 4-6.

NOTE: The fish will *not* be raw, even though it has not been cooked. It's the enzymes in the lime juice that do the "cooking." Be sure to use fresh lime juice; see to it that the strips of fish are completely covered and that they are marinated until the fish turns white.

LOBSTER RING

1 tablespoon (1 envelope) unflavored gelatin
½ cup hot water
2 cans (5 ounces each) lobster
2 tablespoons tarragon vinegar
½ teaspoon coarse salt
½ teaspoon dry mustard

2 tablespoons cut parsley
2 tablespoons chopped onion
¼ cup chopped celery
½ cup chopped cucumber
1 cup heavy cream, whipped

Into the blender, put the gelatin and hot water. Blend at high speed for 30 seconds. Pick over lobster and add with vinegar, salt, mustard, parsley, and onion to blender. Blend at high speed for 30 seconds. Add celery and cucumber and blend at low speed for 10 seconds. Whip cream with whisk or beater, and fold in lobster mixture. Turn into ring mold which has been rinsed with cold water. Chill until firm. Unmold on a large plate lined with Boston lettuce leaves, and fill center with black olives, cherry tomatoes, or mayonnaise mixed with sour cream and chives. Serves 6.

OYSTERS LAFITTE

24 oysters	½ cup cream
¼ cup butter	½ cup grated Parmesan cheese
½ cup chopped onion	
1 tablespoon minced parsley	½ teaspoon coarse salt
¼ cup lemon juice	Freshly ground black pepper

Drain oysters. In a medium skillet, melt the butter. Sauté onion until soft. Add oysters with parsley and cook until edges of oysters curl. Add lemon juice, cream, cheese, salt, and pepper. Heat, but do not boil. Serve with crusty bread. Serves 3-4.

SALMON MOUSSE

This is a marvelous dish for lunch, supper, or even a knockout hors d'oeuvre. I make it whenever I have any baked leftover fish. The recipe calls for 2 cups of fish, so I flake the leftover fish in a 2-cup measure and, if necessary, add canned salmon to make up the 2 cups. It's equally good made with salmon alone.

2 tablespoons (2 envelopes) unflavored gelatin	2 cans (7½ ounces each) salmon
½ cup hot clam broth	1 cup light cream
1 tablespoon lemon juice	½ teaspoon Worcestershire sauce
2 tablespoons chopped onion	4 turns freshly ground pepper
	1 heaping cup crushed ice

Into the blender put the gelatin, hot clam broth, lemon juice, and onion. Cover and blend at high speed for 40 seconds. Pick over salmon and add with packing liquid to blender. Blend at high speed for 5 seconds. With motor on, add cream with Worcestershire and pepper. With motor still on, add crushed ice. When the ice disappears, turn off the motor. Turn into a quart mold which has been rinsed in cold water. Chill until firm (this should happen within 30 minutes). Unmold on a bed of crisp greens; garnish with sliced cucumber, tomato, and fresh dill. Serve with mayonnaise (see p. 145). Serves 4-6.

NORMA'S SALMON IN SHELLS

The friend who contributed several recipes to this book calls this her emergency dish. There is always a can of salmon on hand in her pantry, and she adds whatever else is handy— diced celery, canned sliced mushrooms, chopped scallions, sliced black olives, green pepper, or pimiento.

1 can (7½ ounces) salmon
1 can (8 ounces) tiny peas
1 small onion, minced
3 tablespoons mayonnaise
1 tablespoon lemon juice

1 teaspoon minced fresh dill *or*
½ teaspoon dill weed
½ teaspoon coarse salt
Freshly ground pepper
Minced parsley

Flake the salmon with liquid into a small bowl. Drain the peas and add with onion, may-

onnaise, lemon, dill, salt, and pepper. Pile into
individual baking shells; sprinkle with parsley.
Heat in moderate (350 degree) oven until bubbling. Serves 3.

BROILED SCALLOPS WITH WINE

1½ pounds scallops
¼ cup dry white
  wine*
¼ cup olive oil
1 clove garlic,
  crushed

½ teaspoon salt
Dash of paprika
1 lemon, thinly
  sliced

Try to get bay scallops—they are small and
sweet. If they are not available, use sea scallops, but cut them in half. Marinate the scallops in the remaining ingredients, in a covered
bowl, in the refrigerator for at least 2 hours.
Take the scallops out of the marinade and arrange in a single layer in a shallow baking
dish. Broil for 3-4 minutes, then turn and broil
for 3-4 minutes more, until cooked through.
Serves 4.
*Dry vermouth is an excellent alternative.

SHRIMP-CHEESE BAKE

6 slices white bread
2½ cups (10-ounce
  package) cooked
  shrimp
½ pound Swiss or
  Gruyère cheese,
  grated

¼ cup butter
2 eggs, slightly
  beaten
1 cup milk
1 teaspoon coarse
  salt
½ teaspoon dry mus-
  tard

Cut bread into cubes. Layer bread cubes, shrimp, and grated cheese into a buttered oven-proof casserole. Dot with butter. Mix slightly beaten eggs with milk, salt, and mustard. Pour over bread-shrimp-cheese mixture. Cover and refrigerate for at least 1 hour. Heat in a moderate (350 degree) oven until firm—about 30 minutes. Serves 4.

SHRIMP CURRY

I like a mild curry, and this one is easy and good. I've made it with chicken, leftover lamb, and lobster, as well as the shrimp, with great success. Sometimes I leave the raisins out of the sauce and serve them in a small bowl, along with chutney, cocoanut, and chopped peanuts.

2½ cups (10-ounce package) cooked shrimp

2 cans (10½ ounces each) cream of celery soup

1-3 teaspoons curry powder*

1 individual package (1½ ounces—⅓ cup) plumped raisins†

1 tart unpeeled apple, cubed

In a medium saucepan, combine shrimp, soup (undiluted), curry, and raisins. Heat until bubbling. Add cubed apple and heat for 5 minutes. Serve over rice. Serves 6.

*Add 1 teaspoon curry and taste. This is enough for me, but if you prefer a stronger curry taste, use more.
†To plump the raisins, cover with boiling water. Let stand for a moment or two, then drain.

SHRIMP SEVICHE

1 pound large shrimp	2 tablespoons butter
½ cup fresh lime juice	or oil
2 teaspoons coarse	1 clove garlic, crushed
salt	

Wash the shrimp, but leave them in their shells. Split them up the back with sharp-pointed scissors or knife, and rinse out the black veins. Turn the shrimp into a shallow bowl and cover with lime juice. Sprinkle with salt, cover tightly, and marinate for at least 3 hours. (The lime juice will partially cook the shrimp.) At serving time, heat the butter or oil with the crushed garlic clove. Sauté shrimp for 2 minutes on each side, or until shell turns pink. Serve with lime wedges. Serves 2 for dinner, more for a hot hors d'oeuvre.

SHRIMPERS 'N' RICE

½ pound cooked shrimp (1½ cups)	¼ teaspoon oregano
1 can (1 pound) Spanish rice	2 tablespoons freshly grated Parmesan cheese
¼ cup canned marinara sauce	

Combine shrimp, rice, marinara sauce, and oregano. Turn into a 1½ quart oven-proof casserole. Sprinkle with Parmesan cheese. Heat in a moderate (350 degree) oven until bubbling. Serves 3.

NOTE: You can heat this excellent dish on top of the stove. Add the Parmesan cheese with the remaining ingredients, turn into a medium saucepan and heat over a low flame until bubbling. In either case, don't heat for too long, as overcooking toughens shrimp.

QUICK TUNA CASSEROLE

This was my very first quick recipe—made with potato chips for my brother when I was sixteen. He has never stopped complaining about it, but as I recall, he ate it and asked for seconds. This version is more sophisticated and has a rather exotic, Chinese flavor, but it's still quick and can be made right in the casserole dish out of ingredients that are likely to be on hand.

1 can (7 ounces) tuna fish, drained
1 can (10½ ounces) cream of mushroom soup
1 can (4 ounces) sliced mushrooms, drained
1 package (3 ounces —¾ cup) whole cashew nuts
¼ cup chopped onion
¼ cup chopped celery
2 teaspoons soy sauce
½ teaspoon Worcestershire sauce
1 tablespoon sherry
1 cup Chinese noodles
½ cup sliced pitted ripe olives

In a medium oven-proof casserole, combine the tuna, soup, mushrooms, cashews, onion, celery, soy sauce, Worcestershire, and sherry. Add ¾ cup of the noodles and the sliced olives and mix gently. Crush the remaining

¼ cup of the noodles and sprinkle over the
top. Heat in a moderate (350 degree) oven
until bubbling, about 30 minutes. Serves 4.

Poultry

One of the many things I have learned from my convenience-minded daughters is the marvelous adaptability of the chicken and turkey roast. This excellent product, which is generally available, is boned and rolled. The directions for roasting are simple and clear, and the results are fabulous. If you like firm chicken or turkey easily cubed or sliced for salads, sandwiches, or casseroles, with no waste, you'll become addicted to these packaged roasts. I have used them for all the dishes in this book which call for cubed cooked chicken or turkey.

Ready-cooked barbecued chickens and ducklings are also convenient for a variety of dishes. There are several recipes here, but the possibilities are endless. Almost any favorite chicken recipe can be tailored to accommodate barbecued chicken—the trick is to drastically cut the cooking time.

One word of caution. Beware of barbecued turkeys, unless you are absolutely sure they are cooked through. All poultry can carry the salmonella microbe (which causes a form of food poisoning), and only thorough cooking destroys it. Because of the size of the turkey, and commercial methods of barbecuing, there is always some doubt about its safety.

ASPARAGUS-CHICKEN CASSEROLE

1 can (1 pound)
asparagus spears
1 cup cubed cooked
chicken
1 cup cubed cooked
ham
1 can (10½ ounces)
cheddar cheese
soup

¼ cup sour cream
2 tablespoons
chopped chives
2 tablespoons grated
Parmesan cheese

Drain the asparagus spears and arrange them in a shallow baking dish. Cover with cubed chicken and ham. Mix cheddar cheese soup with sour cream and chives and spoon over the chicken and ham. Sprinkle with freshly grated Parmesan cheese. Heat in a moderate (350 degree) oven until bubbling. Serves 4.

AUDREY'S HONEY-GLAZED CHICKEN

This is my friend Audrey's standby when she has been out all afternoon, and her family is waiting for dinner. It couldn't be simpler, and it's delicious. For variety, try it with orange marmalade instead of honey.

1 barbecued chicken,
quartered
¼ cup butter
½ cup honey

Arrange chicken, skin side up, in a disposable aluminum foil baking pan. Top each quarter with a pat of butter, then drizzle the honey over all. Heat in a moderate (350 degree) oven until butter melts and chicken is glazed, approximately 15 minutes. Serves 3-4.

BAKED CHICKEN WITH HAM

2 cups cubed cooked chicken
2 cups cubed cooked ham
1 can (10½ ounces) mushroom gravy
¼ cup dry white wine
½ cup chopped onion
1 can (4 ounces) sliced mushrooms, drained
1 clove garlic, crushed
¼ teaspoon coarse salt
Freshly ground black pepper

Alternate layers of chicken and ham in a medium baking dish. In a small bowl, mix the gravy, wine, onion, mushrooms, garlic, salt, and pepper. Pour over chicken and ham. Heat in a moderate (350 degree) oven for 30 minutes or until bubbling. Serves 6.

CHICKEN AND ARTICHOKES

2 cups cubed cooked chicken
1 can (8 ounces) artichoke hearts, drained
1 can (10½ ounces) chicken gravy
¼ cup sour cream
2 tablespoons lemon juice
1 tablespoon sherry
½ teaspoon coarse salt
Freshly ground pepper

In a medium saucepan, combine chicken, artichoke hearts, chicken gravy, sour cream, lemon juice, sherry, salt, and pepper. Stir gently until smooth. Heat until beginning to boil. Serve on rice, hot buttered toast, or in heated patty shells. Serves 4.

QUICK CHICKEN CACCIATORE

This is adapted from my regular Chicken Cacciatore recipe. The only difference is that in the standard version the raw chicken is browned, added to the sauce, and cooked for one hour. Here, the addition of tomatoes and spices to the prepared marinara sauce makes it taste as if it had simmered for hours.

2 tablespoons olive oil	marjoram
1 clove garlic, minced	2 tomatoes, cubed
1 cup chopped onion	1 cup canned marinara sauce
1 cup chopped green pepper	1 teaspoon coarse salt
1 tablespoon minced parsley	Freshly ground black pepper
¼ teaspoon each oregano, thyme, and	1 barbecued chicken, cut in eighths

In a medium skillet with a tight-fitting cover, heat the olive oil with garlic, onion, and green pepper until soft. Add parsley, oregano, thyme, marjoram, cubed tomatoes, marinara sauce, salt, and pepper. Add chicken pieces, cover, and cook over low heat for 10 to 15 minutes. Serves 3-4.

CHICKEN WITH CHERRIES

1 barbecued chicken, warm
1 can (1 pound) pitted black cherries
¾ cup chicken broth
1 large clove garlic, crushed
2 tablespoons sherry
¼ teaspoon marjoram

Cut the chicken into eighths and arrange on serving platter. Combine cherries, with juice, and remaining ingredients in a medium saucepan and heat (but do not boil). Pour over chicken or serve in a gravy boat. Serves 3-4.
NOTE: Sauce is thin, but absolutely delicious. If you prefer a slightly thickened sauce, pour a little of the hot liquid into a small dish with 1 teaspoon of cornstarch or finely sifted flour. Mix until smooth, then add slowly to hot sauce, stirring until smooth and thick.

CHICKEN BREASTS WITH TARRAGON

2 whole chicken breasts
¼ cup flour
1 teaspoon coarse salt
Freshly ground black pepper
¼ cup butter
1 tablespoon chopped shallots or onion
1 teaspoon chopped fresh tarragon or
½ teaspoon dried tarragon
¼ cup dry white wine
½ cup chicken broth

Have your butcher bone and halve the
chicken breasts. Remove the skin. Place the
chicken breasts between slices of waxed paper
and pound with a mallet until thin. On a large
piece of aluminum foil, mix the flour with salt
and pepper. Dredge the chicken with seasoned
flour. In a medium skillet, melt the butter. Add
the chicken and brown on both sides. Push to
one side and sauté the shallots or onion until
soft. Add the tarragon, wine, and broth, cover,
and cook until tender, about 10 to 15 minutes.
Serves 3-4.

Oven-fried Chicken I and II

*I prepared two recipes for Oven-Fried
Chicken at the same time so that my family
could help me pick the favorite. Since the vote
was split right down the middle, here are both
versions.*

OVEN-FRIED CHICKEN I

1 medium fryer, cut in eighths	black pepper
2 cups milk	½ cup (about) melted butter
1 teaspoon coarse salt	1 cup finely ground almonds
Freshly ground	

Marinate the chicken pieces in milk. Drain
and pat dry with paper towels. Rub with salt
and pepper. Dip in melted butter, then roll in
ground almonds. Place the pieces without
touching in a buttered shallow glass baking

dish. Sprinkle with any remaining butter—if you've used it all, dot with an additional 2 tablespoons of cold butter. Bake in a hot (400 degree) oven for 1 hour or until very crisp. Serves 3-4.

OVEN-FRIED CHICKEN II

1 medium fryer, cut in eighths
2 cups buttermilk
1 teaspoon coarse salt
Freshly ground pepper
½ cup (about) melted butter
1 clove garlic, crushed
¼ teaspoon paprika
1 cup flour
1 cup freshly grated Parmesan cheese

Marinate the chicken pieces in buttermilk. Drain and pat dry with paper towels. Rub with salt and pepper. Dip into melted butter which has been mixed with the crushed garlic and paprika. Then roll in a mixture of flour and cheese. Place the pieces without touching in a buttered shallow glass baking dish. Sprinkle with any remaining butter—if you've used it all, dot with an additional 2 tablespoons of cold butter. Bake in a hot (400 degree) over for 1 hour or until brown and crisp. Serves 3-4.

CHICKEN VERONIQUE

Here, and in several other recipes in this section, is illustrated the magic in a can of chicken, or beef, or mushroom gravy. With some red or white wine, sour cream, heavy cream, some freshly grated Parmesan cheese, even a bit of currant jelly, you can transform a pedestrian sauce into a culinary triumph.

1 barbecued chicken, warm	½ teaspoon coarse salt
1 can (10½ ounces) chicken gravy	Freshly ground pepper
¼ cup white wine	1 can (8 ounces) seedless grapes, drained
1 clove garlic, crushed	

Keep the chicken warm on a serving platter. In a small saucepan, combine gravy, wine, garlic, salt, and pepper. Heat until beginning to boil. Add drained grapes and stir just enough to heat the grapes through. Pour over chicken, or serve in a gravy boat. Serves 3-4.

TURKEY AND WILD RICE

I tasted this dish originally at La Baroque, a delightful French restaurant in New York. This is a simplified version in which I have tried to duplicate the delicate flavor. I serve it with braised endive (see p. 157) and Fruit Salad Mold (see p. 127).

1 can (14 ounces) cooked wild rice	⅓ cup white raisins, plumped*
3 cups cubed cooked turkey	1 can (10½ ounces) beef or chicken gravy
1 can (4 ounces) broiled mushrooms, drained	½ cup sour cream
	2 tablespoons sherry

| 1 teaspoon coarse salt | Freshly ground black pepper |

Combine the wild rice, turkey, mushrooms, and raisins in a medium oven-proof casserole. In a medium bowl, blend the gravy, sour cream, sherry, salt, and pepper until smooth. Pour over turkey and wild rice. Heat in a moderate (350 degree) oven until piping hot, about 20 minutes. Serves 4.

*To plump the raisins, pour boiling water over them, let stand for a minute or two, then drain.

DUCKLING IN ORANGE SAUCE

1 roasted duckling	1 tablespoon Cointreau
1 can (10½ ounces) chicken gravy	1 can (11 ounces) mandarin orange sections
¼ cup red wine	
2 tablespoons red currant jelly	

Keep the duckling warm on a serving platter. Combine the gravy and red wine in a small skillet. Add currant jelly and Cointreau and stir until the gravy begins to boil. Drain the orange sections, add, and heat. Pour over the duckling and serve immediately. Serves 4-5.

CHICKEN LIVERS SAUTE

¼ cup butter
½ cup chopped
  onion
½ pound sliced
  mushrooms
  (about 1 cup)
1 pound chicken
  livers

2-3 tablespoons dry
  vermouth
1 teaspoon coarse
  salt
¼ teaspoon dried
  rosemary
Freshly ground
  black pepper

In a large skillet, melt the butter. Add the chopped onion, sliced mushrooms, and drained chicken livers and sauté for 5 minutes. Add vermouth with salt, rosemary, and black pepper, and cook until livers are done. They should be brown on the outside but still pink inside. Serve immediately on rice, noodles, or toast points. Serves 3-4.

MEAT

When it comes to quick meat products, the choice is rather circumscribed. There are some canned meats that taste good—ham, tongue, chipped beef—but others, like hamburgers in gravy, are just not worth trying. And the frozen food industry has not progressed any further in this area than TV dinners.

Of course, frankfurters and most sausages require no cooking, and they add variety to quick meat recipes. You'll find several that use them here. If you're lucky enough to have a gourmet food shop in your neighborhood, browse around the prepared meat counter for sausages of all types and origins.

The next time you're in a hurry, you might try some slices of cooked ham, tongue, or roast beef from your favorite delicatessen. With the addition of a well-seasoned sauce or gravy, (recipes for some of these are included in the chapter on sauces), you can put together a quick dinner your family will applaud.

Hamburger cooks quickly from scratch, and we have included an outstanding meat loaf, a hamburger supreme, and a steak tartare to start you thinking. And the veal chop recipes should give you flavorful chops without preliminary browning.

QUICK BEEF STROGANOFF

1½ pounds fillet of beef	1 cup chopped onion
1 teaspoon coarse salt	1 tablespoon flour
Freshly ground black pepper	1 cup beef broth
	½ teaspoon Dijon mustard
¼ cup butter	¼ cup sour cream

Remove fat and gristle from meat, and cut into narrow strips. Add salt and pepper to meat, and refrigerate. In a medium skillet, melt 2 tablespoons of the butter. Add chopped onion and cook until soft. Add flour and beef broth, and stir over medium heat until thickened and smooth. Add mustard. In another skillet, melt the remaining 2 tablespoons of butter. Add the meat strips and brown quickly on both sides. Add to sauce with sour cream and heat, but do not boil (or the cream will curdle). Serve immediately over noodles or rice. Serves 4.

BAKED HAMBURGERS

1 pound ground round steak	¼ cup freshly grated Parmesan cheese
1 teaspoon coarse salt	2 tablespoons chopped scallions or shallots
Freshly ground black pepper	4 large pitted black olives

Lightly toss hamburger meat with salt, pepper, cheese, and scallions or shallots. Shape into 4 patties. Stuff each one with a pitted black olive. Arrange on a foil tray. Bake in a hot (425 degree) oven—10 minutes for rare hamburgers, 15 minutes for medium-rare, 20 minutes for well done. Serves 2-3. Of course these can be oven or pan broiled.

SPEEDY MEAT LOAF

2 slices white bread
½ cup milk
1 egg, slightly beaten
¼ cup dehydrated onion soup mix
¼ cup minced fresh parsley
1 clove garlic, crushed
1 teaspoon coarse salt
Freshly ground black pepper
½ teaspoon Dijon mustard
1 pound ground chuck

Tear the bread into small pieces. Mix with milk and egg; let stand while you assemble the remaining ingredients. Add onion soup mix, parsley, garlic, salt, pepper, and mustard to the ground beef. Add milk mixture and mix lightly. Shape into a loaf and place on a buttered shallow baking dish (or disposable foil pan). Heat in a moderate (350 degree) oven about 50 minutes. Serves 4.

STEAK TARTARE

There are as many versions of Steak Tartare as there are cooks who make it. This is my favorite, but I have tasted many others that were outstanding. The only thing I am finicky about is the meat. You'll find instructions for your butcher below.

1 pound lean steak, ground twice*	¼ teaspoon sweet Hungarian paprika
¼ cup chopped onion	¼ teaspoon Worcestershire sauce
2 tablespoons capers	
1 teaspoon coarse salt	
Freshly ground pepper	1 tablespoon sherry or cognac, if desired
	1 egg yolk

Lightly mix the ground beef with the seasonings. Add sherry or cognac if desired. Mound the meat on a serving platter, make an indentation in the top and drop in the egg yolk. Garnish with chopped parsley or chives and serve with thinly sliced buttered toast or black bread. Serves 2-3.

*Be sure to tell your butcher you are serving the meat raw. Ask him to see to it that your ground steak is completely free of fat, and that it is absolutely fresh.

BROILED LAMB CHOPS

8 loin lamb chops	1 tablespoon lemon juice
2 tablespoons Dijon mustard	1 clove garlic, crushed
1 tablespoon anchovy paste	¼ teaspoon oregano

Preheat the broiler. In a shallow foil pan, arrange the lamb chops. In a small bowl or jar, mix the mustard, anchovy paste, lemon juice,

crushed garlic, and oregano. Spread half of
mustard mixture on the lamb chops. Broil the
chops for about 5 minutes or until brown.
Turn the chops and spread with remaining mustard mixture. Broil for 4 to 5 minutes or until
brown on the outside but still pink inside.
Serve immediately. Serves 4.

VEAL WITH LEMON

1 pound veal,
Italian style
⅓ cup flour
1½ teaspoons coarse
salt
Freshly ground
black pepper
3 tablespoons
butter
¼ cup chicken stock
2 tablespoons dry
vermouth
2 tablespoons
lemon juice
1 tablespoon
chopped scallions
1 tablespoon
minced parsley
2 sprigs fresh
rosemary
1 lemon, cut in
paper-thin slices

Cut the veal into 3-inch squares. On a large
piece of foil, mix the flour with salt and pepper. Dip the veal into the seasoned flour. In a
large skillet, melt the butter. Brown the veal
over a moderately high flame; turn and brown
the other side. Add the chicken stock, vermouth, lemon juice, scallions, parsley, rosemary, and lemon slices. Cover and simmer
gently for 3-4 minutes or until cooked through.
Serves 3-4.

VEAL WITH BLACK OLIVES

1 pound veal, Italian style	1 clove garlic, minced
⅓ cup flour	1 tablespoon tomato purée
1½ teaspoons coarse salt	½ cup chicken stock
Freshly ground black pepper	½ cup sliced pitted black olives
2 tablespoons butter	¼ cup freshly grated Parmesan cheese
2 tablespoons olive oil	¼ teaspoon oregano

Cut the veal into 3-inch squares. On a large piece of foil, mix the flour with salt and pepper. Dip the veal squares into the seasoned flour. In a large skillet, heat the butter with the olive oil. Add the minced garlic. Brown the veal over a moderately high flame; turn and brown the other side. Stir the tomato purée into the chicken stock. Add to the veal with the olives, cheese, and oregano. Cover and simmer gently for 3-4 minutes or until the veal is cooked through. Serves 3-4.

BRAISED VEAL CHOPS

3 tablespoons butter	4 veal chops
½ cup chopped onion	1 teaspoon coarse salt
½ cup chopped green pepper	Freshly ground black pepper
1 clove garlic, minced	½ cup chicken stock
1 tablespoon capers	¼ cup sour cream

Melt the butter over low heat in an oven-proof casserole with a lid. Add onion, green pepper, and garlic and cook until soft. Add capers. Arrange veal chops over this mixture; sprinkle with salt and pepper. Pour chicken stock over the top. Cover the casserole and put into a moderately hot (375 degree) oven. Cook for 1 hour or until veal chops are cooked through. Remove chops to serving platter, add sour cream to juices in casserole, blend, pour over veal chops, and serve. Serves 2-3.

PATTI'S CASSEROLE

My daughter Patti doesn't like to cook. She doesn't even like to eat meat. But this is her favorite dish, and I make it whenever she comes home from college. She likes it best with broad noodles, but it's good with red or white beans, corn, lima beans, or rice.

3 tablespoons butter	2 cups cooked noodles
½ cup chopped onion	
1 clove garlic, minced	1 teaspoon coarse salt
1 pound ground chuck or round steak	Freshly ground black pepper
	½ cup sour cream
1 cup canned marinara sauce	

Melt the butter in a large skillet. Add onion and garlic, and cook until soft. Add ground beef and crumble with a fork; stir until meat loses its redness. Stir in marinara sauce, noodles, salt and pepper. Just before serving time, add sour cream and heat but do not boil. Serves 4.

HAM WITH CURRANT GLAZE

1 ham slice, 1½ inches thick (about 2 pounds) Whole cloves	½ teaspoon dry mustard
½ cup currant jelly	¼ teaspoon ground cinnamon
1 tablespoon vinegar	Dash of ground cloves

Place the ham slice in a disposable aluminum baking dish. Dot with whole cloves. Place in a moderate (350 degree) oven for 15 minutes. Beat the jelly with a fork until somewhat liquid. Add vinegar, mustard, cinnamon, and a dash of ground cloves. Spoon over the ham and bake for 20 minutes or until glazed. Serves 4.

ORANGE-GLAZED HAM

1 can (1 pound) cooked ham Whole cloves	¼ teaspoon dry mustard
	½ cup orange marmalade

Turn the ham into an aluminum foil baking pan. With a sharp pointed knife, score the skin into diamonds; stud each diamond with a clove. Sprinkle with dry mustard. Top with orange marmalade. Heat in a moderate (350

degree) oven for 20-30 minutes or until bubbling and glazed. Serves 3.

TONGUE AND HAM WITH MUSHROOMS

1 pound cooked   mushrooms
  beef tongue   ½ teaspoon Dijon
½ pound cooked ham   mustard
1 can (10½ ounces)   ¼ cup freshly grated
  mushroom gravy   Parmesan cheese
¼ cup white wine   2 tablespoons
1 can (4 ounces)   minced parsley
  chopped

Slice tongue and ham, and arrange alternat-
ing slices in a shallow oven-proof dish. Combine gravy, wine, drained chopped mushrooms, and mustard. Pour over tongue and
ham. Combine cheese and parsley and sprinkle
over all. Heat under the broiler (but not too
close to the flame) for about 10 minutes, or
until cheese melts and meat is heated through.
Serves 4-6.

EASY CHOUCROUTE

*If you like provincial French cooking, this
dish and the next should please you. They
are made with humble ingredients like sauerkraut and sausage, but they have a marvelous
hearty taste. Look for sauerkraut in plastic
bags. It's not as readily available as canned
sauerkraut, but somehow it tastes better. Your*

*butcher may stock it. If you must use the
canned, be sure to drain and rinse thoroughly
in a sieve under cold running water.*

2 bags or 2 cans (1
  pound each)
  sauerkraut
1 cup diced cooked
  ham
1 clove garlic,
  minced
1 cup chopped onion
  Freshly ground

black pepper
Dash of ground
  cloves
1 cup dry white wine
1 pound Polish
  (garlic) sausage
4 knockwurst or
  frankfurters

Drain the sauerkraut, wash it in cold water,
and squeeze out all the liquid. Mix it with the
diced ham, garlic, onion, pepper, and cloves in
a heavy saucepan with a tight-fitting cover.
Add the wine. It should cover the sauerkraut.
If it doesn't, or if it cooks away, add more
wine or chicken broth. Cover and simmer for
at least 30 minutes. Add Polish sausage and
cook 30 minutes more. Add knockwurst 20
minutes before serving, or frankfurters 5
minutes before serving. Choucroute should
simmer on a low flame all during the cooking.
Serves 4.

NOTE: You can vary this dish by adding or
substituting many kinds of sausage—thick
slices of salami, Italian sweet or hot sausage,
Danish or German sausage. If you prefer, you
can brown the meat in a skillet before you
cook it in the sauerkraut, but I prefer this
method.

KNOCKWURST AND SAUERKRAUT IN BEER

1 bag or can (1   6 knockwurst
  pound) sauerkraut   ¼ cup beer
½ teaspoon caraway
  seeds

Turn sauerkraut into a medium skillet. Add
caraway seeds and combine. Place the knockwurst on the sauerkraut. Pour beer over
all. Cover and heat slowly until piping hot.
Add more beer, if necessary. Serve with hot
mustard and mugs of icy cold beer. Serves 3.

FRANKFURTER CASSEROLE

2 cans (1 pound   8 frankfurters
  each) lima beans   2 tablespoons
½ cup chopped onion   butter
¼ cup chili sauce

Drain one can of the lima beans. Turn both
cans into an oven-proof casserole with the
chopped onion and chili sauce. Arrange the
frankfurters around the top of the casserole.
Dot with butter. Bake in a moderate (350 degree) oven for about 40 minutes, or until casserole is piping hot and liquid is almost all
absorbed. Serves 4.

SWEET AND SOUR FRANKFURTERS

1 can (1 pound) whole cranberry sauce	1 bottle chili sauce 8-10 frankfurters

Combine the cranberry and chili sauces in a medium saucepan. Heat and add frankfurters. Cover and simmer until frankfurters are heated through. Serves 4-5.

NOTE: Use cocktail frankfurters for hors d'oeuvres. This sauce is also marvelous with meatballs. Use tiny ones for parties and regular-sized meatballs for family meals, but be sure that the larger meatballs are cooked through.

ROAST BEEF ROLLS

8 slices rare roast beef	1 teaspoon horseradish
1 package (8 ounces) cream cheese	2 tablespoons minced parsley
¼ cup Roquefort cheese	1 tablespoon milk or cream

Spread out the slices of roast beef. Mix cheeses with horseradish, parsley, and cream or milk. Spread on roast beef slices. Roll the slices and wrap in plastic wrap. Chill until serving time. For hors d'oeuvres, cut the rolls into 1 inch slices. For a main course, place 2 rolls on each plate, garnish with parsley, and serve with crusty baked beans, buttered French bread, and a crisp vegetable salad. Serves 4.

SECOND-DAY STEAK

2 cups (about) cooked rare steak
2 tablespoons olive oil
2 tablespoons butter
1 clove garlic, minced
½ cup chopped onion
½ cup chopped green pepper
1 teaspoon flour
1 cup chicken stock
1 tablespoon soy sauce
1 tablespoon Marsala wine

Slice the steak thin. In a medium saucepan melt the olive oil and butter. Sauté the garlic, onion, and green pepper until soft. Transfer to a small bowl. Toss in sliced steak and heat quickly. Transfer the steak to a hot plate. Turn the onion mixture back into the saucepan, sprinkle with flour, and then stir in chicken stock, soy sauce, and Marsala. Stir and cook quickly until the mixture boils. Pour over steak and serve immediately. Serves 3-4.

QUICK CASSOULET

This recipe looks long and complicated, but it is really simple to make. There are many ingredients, but that's the nature of a cassoulet. The classic recipe is made with lamb and duck, but this one uses ground beef to save time. You'll find it takes a few minutes to assemble the cassoulet and pop it into the oven. And what comes out is company fare!

1 tablespoon butter
½ pound sweet Italian sausage
½ pound Polish (garlic) sausage
1 cup chopped onion
2 cloves garlic, sliced
1 pound ground round steak
1 tablespoon course salt
8 turns freshly ground black pepper
2 cans (20 ounces each) cannellini (white kidney beans)
½ cup dry white wine
1 tablespoon tomato purée
½ cup chicken or beef broth
½ teaspoon dried thyme
¼ cup flavored bread crumbs

In a large skillet, melt the butter. Sauté the sliced sweet and garlic sausages, and the chopped onion and garlic. Add the ground round steak and stir until the meat loses its redness. Add salt and pepper. Drain the white beans, reserving the liquid. Arrange one can of the beans in a large oven-proof casserole. Top with half of the meat mixture. Add the second can of beans and the remaining meat. In the same skillet, heat the wine with the tomato purée, broth, thyme, and ½ cup of the reserved bean liquid. When it is bubbling, pour it over the casserole. Sprinkle bread crumbs over all. Heat in a moderately hot (375 degree) oven for 1 hour. Serves 6-8.

LIVER WITH SOUR CREAM

1½ pounds sliced calf's liver	1 teaspoon coarse salt
4 tablespoons flour	¼ teaspoon paprika
¼ cup butter	Freshly ground black pepper
1 cup sour cream	
2 tablespoons sherry	

Dredge the sliced liver with flour. In a large skillet, melt the butter. Sauté the liver quickly, 1 to 2 minutes on each side. Add sour cream, sherry, salt, paprika and pepper. Stir and cook until heated through, but do not boil. Serves 4.

NOTE: I have made this dish with avocado cubes, and it's excellent. Just peel half an avocado and cut into cubes. Add to the liver with the sour cream.

Cooperative Cookery

Like a good executive, I love to delegate authority. When my husband expertly grills and carves a butterfly leg of lamb, I'm happy and proud of his proficiency. When I see my guests spearing and cooking their meat at the table, I realize that they are having a good time. And when the end result of all this participation means less work for mother, I wonder why we don't do all our entertaining on a cooperative basis.

Charcoal grilling is a suburban phenomenon, but it is much more than that. From the first forays with hot dogs and hamburgers to the eight sophisticated recipes in this chapter, you have the evolution of charcoal cooking from a novelty to a culinary art.

Fondues are great fun, for hosts and guests alike. Aside from the initial expense—fondue pots, burners, and long-handled forks—they are easy to prepare for. And the fact that everyone participates makes for a gay, informal party.

THE CHARCOAL GRILL

JOAN'S GRILLED HAMBURGER

A friend of mine, who is famous for her outdoor parties, always serves hamburger, and this is her recipe. She insists that the secret of her success is not in the mixture of ingredients, but in the meat. She has her butcher grind it less than an hour before the party. She makes very large patties (three to a pound), broils them quickly, and serves them with sliced beefsteak tomatoes and sweet onion.

2 pounds ground
round steak or
sirloin
2 teaspoons coarse
salt
Freshly ground
pepper
2 tablespoons grated
onion
2 tablespoons butter

Lightly toss beef with salt, pepper, and grated onion. Form into six large balls. Flatten them slightly and place on grill 3 to 4 inches from the hot coals. Cook about 5 minutes on each side for rare hamburgers, more if you like them better done. When the hamburgers are almost finished, dot with a teaspoonful of butter. Serve immediately on a hot platter with heated rolls. Serves 3-4.

BARBECUED SPARERIBS

3 pounds spareribs
1 bottle (12 ounces)
  tomato ketchup

1 jar (10 ounces)
  guava jelly

Spareribs require long, slow cooking—if you start them on charcoal, they will have to be cooked for 1 to 1½ hours. To speed up the cooking time, you can parboil them for 30 minutes, and then grill them over the coals for 15 minutes more or until crisp and brown. Place the spareribs about 5 inches from the hot coals. Beat the ketchup and jelly together with a fork until smooth, and brush on spareribs while cooking. Turn and baste frequently until ribs are crisp, glazed, and tender. Use remaining sauce at the table. Serves 4.

GRILLED CORN

6 ears of corn
¼ cup butter,
  softened

6 Boston lettuce
  leaves, soaked

Husk the corn thoroughly. Brush each ear with softened butter. Wrap each ear in a wet lettuce leaf, then in aluminum foil. Grill over hot coals for 30 to 40 minues or until cooked through. Turn occasionally. Serves 4-6.

GRILLED BUTTERFLY LAMB

1 leg of lamb (5-6
  pounds)
1 cup red wine
½ cup olive oil
2 tablespoons lemon
  juice
2 cloves garlic,
  sliced

1 teaspoon coarse
  salt
½ teaspoon rosemary
4 turns freshly
  ground black
  pepper

Have your butcher "butterfly" the lamb. He
will cut it from the bone, but not roll it. Cut
away bits of adhering fat; spread out flat in
large baking dish and marinate for several
hours in the wine, oil, lemon, garlic, salt, rosemary, and pepper. Grill the meat on an even
bed of gray coals, with the grill 3 to 4 inches
above the coals. Start it cooking fat side up.
Grill for 15 minutes. Turn and grill for 10
minutes. Cook another 5 minutes on each side,
maneuvering the roast so that the thick portion
is over the hottest part of the fire, and the thin
portion over the cooler area of the grill. The
meat should be pink. Don't be misled by the
charred, misshapen appearance of the meat.
When you carve it in thin slices against the
grain, it will look and taste delicious. Serve
with Avgolemono sauce (see page 142). Serves
6-8.

GRILLED POLYNESIAN CHICKEN

¾ cup soy sauce
¾ cup chili sauce
¾ cup lime
   marmalade

¼ cup honey
2 tablespoons sherry
1 broiling chicken,
   cut in quarters

Combine soy sauce, chili sauce, marmalade, honey, and sherry. Grill the chicken on an even bed of gray coals, with the grill 5 to 6 inches above the coals. Start the chicken skin side up and brush with the soy sauce mixture. Grill the chicken for about 40 minutes, turning every ten minutes and basting with the sauce. The chicken is done when the juice runs yellow, not pink. Serve the chicken with the remaining sauce. Serves 3-4.

NOTE: This method of grilling chicken requires time and patience, but it is the only way to get the charcoal flavor without burned and charred chicken. You can do this chicken in the oven, of course, and baste it with the Polynesian sauce. It will take about 1 hour in a moderately hot oven.

GRILLED FLANK STEAK

1 flank steak (about
   2½ pounds)
¼ cup soy sauce
¼ cup sherry
¼ cup olive oil

1 teaspoon preserved
   ginger, chopped
1 clove garlic,
   minced

Arrange flank steak in shallow dish or tray. Combine soy sauce, sherry, olive oil, ginger, and garlic in a jar and shake. Pour over flank steak and marinate for several hours, turning the steak 2 or 3 times. Grill on a hot fire, with the grill 2 inches from the coals. Baste with the marinade while broiling. Flank steak must be served rare, so turn the steak after 5 minutes on one side. After 4 minutes on the second side, test. Serve the steak on a wooden board, carved in paper-thin diagonal slices. Serves 4.

GRILLED STEAK ROQUEFORT

1 sirloin steak	2 tablespoons cream
Coarse salt	cheese
2 tablespoons butter,	2 tablespoons
softened	Roquefort cheese

Have your butcher cut the steak about 2 inches thick. Sprinkle with coarse salt, and grill it quickly on a bed of gray coals about 2½ inches from the fire. Cook for 5 minutes and turn. When second side is almost done, about 2 minutes, spread mixture of butter, cream cheese, and Roquefort on top, and continue to broil. Serve immediately on hot platter. Serves 4.

GRILLED SWORDFISH

This is probably the best fish dish I have ever tasted. If the steaks are cut thick enough, and all the directions are followed, I guarantee the perfection of the result.

3 pounds swordfish*   ½ cup bourbon
½ cup soy sauce   3 lemons

Marinate the swordfish with the soy sauce and bourbon for several hours. Spoon the marinade over the fish 2 or 3 times. Grill the swordfish steaks on a very hot charcoal fire about 15 minutes on each side. Baste occasionally with the marinade. Cover with a foil shield (we use a disposable foil baking pan) for the last 10 minutes. Serve immediately with lemon wedges. Serves 6.

*Ask your fish dealer to cut the swordfish steaks 1½ inches thick. You will have to tell him at least twice —this seems to be an unusual request.

THE FONDUE

FONDUE BOURGUIGNONNE

I tasted this first in Paris at a restaurant over a cheese store. I assumed what I had ordered was a cheese fondue, and when the raw meat was set before me I was horrified. But then the waiter brought the sizzling oil and all the accoutrements, and showed me how to proceed. I've served this many times since that first memorable encounter, and it's always very special.

3 pounds fillet of beef   2 cups vegetable oil
1 cup (2 sticks) but-
   ter, clarified

Have your butcher cut the beef in 2-inch cubes and trim it. (I've tried this with less expensive cuts of beef—it just doesn't work. You can save money by buying a small whole fillet and using the rest for steaks, hamburgers, or stroganoff.)

To clarify butter, cut sticks in pieces and heat very slowly in small pan. As the butter melts, it separates. The clear fat on top is the clarified butter; the milky sediment at the bottom of the pan can be discarded or used in other dishes.

Half an hour before serving, using two fondue pots, heat the vegetable oil over medium heat; add the clarified butter. (The butter will not smoke—that's why you clarified it.) Keep the oil and butter mixture very hot, but under the boiling point, until serving time. Then raise the heat to bring oil to the boil. Bring sizzling oil to table and set over burner. Serve cubes of raw meat to each guest. Pass a tray of sauces like Béarnaise, Remoulade, Horseradish, Roquefort, or Chutney sauce (see Chapter 8). Give each guest a long wooden-handled fork for cooking his meat, and a standard fork for eating. Serves 6, three to a pot.

DAVID'S RABBIT

⅓ cup beer or ale
½ teaspoon coarse salt
½ teaspoon dry mustard
3 turns freshly ground black pepper

1 tablespoon Worcestershire sauce
1 pound sharp cheddar cheese, cubed
½ teaspoon cream of tartar

In a chafing dish or fondue pot, over low heat, combine beer, salt, mustard, pepper, and

Worcestershire. When beer is hot and beginning to boil, add cubed cheese and cream of tartar. Stir over low heat until melted and smooth. Bring to table and set over burner. Serve with chunks of hot French bread. Serves 4.

MONTEREY JACK

1 tablespoon butter
¼ cup chopped onion
½ pound Monterey Jack cheese*
1 can (1 pound) red kidney beans
2 ripe tomatoes, cubed
¼ cup chopped pimiento or canned sweet roasted pepper
¼ cup white wine
½ teaspoon Worcestershire sauce

In a chafing dish or 2-quart fondue pot, melt the butter over low heat. Add onion and cook until golden. Add cubed cheese and stir until cheese is melted. Add drained beans, cubed tomatoes, pimiento, wine, and Worcestershire. Cook until cheese is the consistency of mayonnaise. Bring to table and set over burner. Serve with hunks of French bread, pumpernickel, or sour rye. Serves 4.

*If you can't find Monterey Jack cheese, use cheddar cheese.

Salads & Salad Dressings

Salad is my favorite food, and I have strong convictions about how it should be served. For one thing, I abhor a salad with too much dressing. The French use barely enough dressing to coat every leaf—as you will notice in the Ground Floor Salad recipe on page 128. If there is a puddle of dressing in the bottom of the bowl, you've used too much.

Another pet peeve is the thick sweet glop that passes for prepared salad dressing. Commercial mayonnaise is really quite good—with a little fixing, it does yeoman service for salads and sauces. But there is no trick I have ever found to make bought salad dressing palatable. And since it takes no time at all to mix olive oil with vinegar and a little seasoning, I can't see its value, even to a quick cook.

A tossed green salad (what the French call *salade simple*) should consist of salad greens (one or more varieties) which have been washed, dried, and torn into bite-sized pieces. If this is done ahead, the salad greens can be refrigerated in a plastic bag; if not, the salad can be prepared right in the bowl. The dressing should be sprinkled sparingly over the greens at the table (not beforehand) and carefully tossed.

When it comes to a *salade composée* (salad with meat, vegetables, fish, eggs, or other ingredients), the same general rules apply. The variety and combination of ingredients, however, is limited only by your imagination.

ARTICHOKE AND ANCHOVY SALAD

1 can (1 pound) artichoke bottoms, drained	1 teaspoon grated onion
2-3 tomatoes, peeled and sliced	1 clove garlic, minced
1 can (2 ounces) anchovy fillets	1 teaspoon chopped parsley
2 tablespoons tarragon wine vinegar	{ 1 sprig tarragon *or* ¼ teaspoon dried tarragon

Arrange the drained artichoke bottoms in a shallow serving dish. Top each artichoke with a slice of tomato. Arrange the anchovy fillets over all, reserving the oil. In a small screw-top jar, combine the oil from the anchovies with vinegar, onion, garlic, parsley, and tarragon. Shake until blended, then pour over and around the anchovies. Marinate, covered, in the refrigerator, for at least 1 hour; the longer it marinates, the better the flavor. Garnish with watercress and black olives. Serves 4-6.

AVOCADOS WITH ANCHOVY DRESSING

1 can (2 ounces) anchovy fillets	¼ cup tomato juice
3 tablespoons olive oil	1 teaspoon grated onion
1 tablespoon red wine vinegar	¼ teaspoon salt Freshly ground pepper
1 tablespoon lemon juice	½ teaspoon sugar
	2 ripe avocados

Drain and mash anchovies. Turn into a screw-top jar with oil, vinegar, lemon juice, tomato juice, onion, salt, pepper, and sugar. Cover and chill until serving time. Peel and quarter the avocados. Arrange individual servings of 2 quarters each on romaine lettuce leaves and sprinkle with anchovy dressing. Serves 4.

NOTE: This dressing may be used on other salads, but it is so piquant that it is the perfect foil for the bland avocado.

Patty's Bean Salad I and II

Patty is a friend with five sons and a husband, a big house and a swimming pool. Here are two salads she serves for lunch around the pool. They are both so hearty and good that I recommend them without reservation.

PATTY'S BEAN SALAD I

1½ cups (about ½ pound) cubed salami	½ cup thinly sliced scallion
1 can (1 pound) whole string beans	½ cup diced celery
	¼ cup olive oil
2 hard-cooked eggs, sliced	2 tablespoons red wine vinegar
½ cup thinly sliced radish	1 teaspoon coarse salt
	Freshly ground pepper

Combine the salami with drained string beans, eggs, radish, scallion, and celery. Add oil, vinegar, salt, and pepper; toss gently. Cover and chill. Serve on Boston lettuce. Serves 4 as a main course, more in a buffet.

PATTY'S BEAN SALAD II

2 cans (1 pound each) whole string beans

1 can (7 ounces) pitted black olives

1 jar (12 ounces) olive condite (salad)

1 jar (4 ounces) sliced pimientos

1 can (4 ounces) sliced mushrooms
  or
1 cup sliced raw mushrooms

1 jar (6 ounces) marinated artichoke hearts

2⁄3 cup olive oil

1⁄3 cup red wine vinegar

1 large clove garlic, crushed

2 teaspoons coarse salt

Freshly ground pepper

Drain and combine the string beans, black olives, condite, pimientos, and mushrooms. Add the artichoke hearts with the marinade. Add oil, vinegar, garlic, salt, and pepper and toss gently to combine. Cover and marinate for several hours or overnight. Drain the marinade and serve on crisp lettuce leaves. Serves 6-8 as a main course, more in a buffet.

BEAN SLAW

1 cup cooked lima beans	¼ cup sliced radishes
½ cup cooked red kidney beans	¼ cup mayonnaise
1 cup shredded cabbage, tightly packed	1 tablespoon red wine vinegar
½ cup thin-sliced red onion rings	½ teaspoon coarse salt
	Freshly ground black pepper

Toss all ingredients lightly together. Chill until serving time. Serves 4.

SAVOY CABBAGE SALAD

Savoy cabbage is a curly-leafed, pale green variety—more tender than regular cabbage and much prettier. Try it in this salad, and any other that calls for green cabbage. It's smashing, too, as a party centerpiece. Cut a slice off the bottom so it sits flat on your serving dish, hollow out the middle to fill with Remoulade Sauce (see p. 148), and surround with shrimp.

2½ cups tightly packed shredded Savoy cabbage	2 tablespoons white wine vinegar
4 tablespoons olive oil	½ teaspoon coarse salt
2 tablespoons sour cream	4 turns freshly ground pepper

In a shallow salad bowl, toss the cabbage with olive oil, sour cream, vinegar, salt, and pepper. Cover and chill until serving time. Serves 4.

NOTE: If you can't find Savoy cabbage, try this salad with very young green cabbage or red cabbage.

CAULIFLOWER SURPRISE SALAD

1½ cups cauliflower, cut in flowerets
2 tablespoons olive oil
2 tablespoons wine vinegar
1 cup watercress
½ cup sliced black olives
½ cup cubed cucumber
¼ cup minced scallions
¼ cup thinly sliced onion rings
2 tablespoons mayonnaise
1 tablespoon sour cream

Marinate the cauliflowerets in oil and vinegar for at least 2 hours. Drain marinade, but do not discard. Add watercress, olives, cucumber, scallions, and onions. In a small dish, mix the mayonnaise with the sour cream and as much of the marinade as you need to make a smooth dressing—about 1 tablespoon. Serves 4.

NOTE: We found the salad perfect the way it is—without additional salt or pepper. Taste it, and if you prefer more seasoning, add it.

CHEF SALAD

6 cups shredded
salad greens
1 cup cooked
chicken, cut in
strips
1 cup cooked ham,
cut in strips
1 cup Swiss cheese,
cut in strips

½ teaspoon coarse
salt
Freshly ground
pepper
1 clove garlic,
crushed
1 egg yolk
½ cup olive oil
2 tablespoons red
wine vinegar

At serving time, arrange the salad greens in a large salad bowl. Add chicken, ham, and cheese. In a small bowl put salt, pepper, and garlic; add egg yolk. Pour in olive oil gradually, beating with a spoon or whisk. Add vinegar slowly, beating all the while. Add dressing at the table, using just enough to coat the ingredients. Toss thoroughly. Serves 4.

CHICKEN IN AVOCADO

2 cups cubed cooked
chicken
1 cup diced celery
1 tablespoon diced
pimiento
¼ cup mayonnaise
2 tablespoons sour
cream
1 tablespoon milk or
cream

2 tablespoons lemon
juice
½ teaspoon coarse
salt
Freshly ground
black pepper
⅛ teaspoon ground
ginger
2 ripe avocados
¼ cup salted almonds

In a medium bowl mix the chicken, celery, pimiento, mayonnaise, sour cream, milk or cream, and 1 tablespoon of the lemon juice. Add salt, pepper, and ginger. Cover and chill until serving time. At serving time, peel and halve the avocados. Sprinkle with remaining lemon juice. Set each half on a bed of romaine and fill with chicken salad. Sprinkle with salted almonds, which may be chopped or slivered but preferably whole. Pass additional French dressing, if desired. Serves 4.

DONNA'S CHICKEN SALAD

2 cups cubed cooked chicken	2 tablespoons wine vinegar
1 cup diced cucumber	1 teaspoon garlic salt
¼ cup mayonnaise	

Toss chicken with cucumber, mayonnaise, and wine vinegar. Add garlic salt. Serve on lettuce with quartered tomatoes and black olives. Serves 3-4.

CRAB SUPREME

This dish is aptly named. I adapted it from a recipe demonstrated on television by a famous French chef. His version included black caviar, but I think that's gilding the lily.

1 pound fresh
crabmeat
¼ cup chopped
chives
¼ cup chopped
parsley
1-2 tablespoons
cognac, if desired

⅓ cup mayonnaise
2 tablespoons lemon
juice
½ teaspoon coarse
salt
Freshly ground
black pepper
2 avocados

Pick over crabmeat to remove any bits of shell or cartilage. Add chives, parsley, cognac (if desired), mayonnaise, lemon juice, salt, and pepper. Peel and halve the avocados, sprinkle with more lemon juice, and place on a bed of romaine. Fill each half with crabmeat mixture. Serves 4.

ITALIAN RICE SALAD

2 cups (1 pint)
cooked white rice
¼ cup chopped green
pepper
¼ cup sliced, pitted
black olives
¼ cup chopped celery
2 tablespoons
chopped red
radishes
¼ cup pignolia nuts

1 teaspoon anchovy
paste
¼ cup olive oil
2 tablespoons lemon
juice
½ teaspoon coarse
salt
Freshly ground
black pepper

In a medium bowl mix the rice, green pepper, olives, celery, radishes, and pignolia nuts. Add anchovy paste with the olive oil and lemon juice, salt, and pepper. Toss lightly and chill until serving time. Serve with cold sliced meat, quiche, or as part of an antipasto assortment. Serves 4.

JANE'S COLE SLAW

Jane is one of my cooking daughters, and the salad expert in the family. I am inclined to use fresh garlic instead of garlic salt, but I never tinker with my daughters' recipes.

3 cups shredded
  cabbage
1 cup grated carrots
1 tablespoon grated
  onion
½ teaspoon garlic salt
½ cup mayonnaise
2 tablespoons red
  wine vinegar

Toss all ingredients until combined. Cover and chill until serving time. Serves 4-6.

OLD-FASHIONED CUCUMBER SALAD

2 cucumbers, peeled
1 medium onion
½ cup olive oil
½ cup wine vinegar
⅔ cup water
5 tablespoons sugar
1 teaspoon salt
Freshly ground
  pepper

Slice the cucumbers (as thin as you can) into a quart jar. Add thinly sliced onion rings, oil, vinegar, water, and seasoning. Close the jar tightly and shake to combine. Refrigerate for several hours or overnight. Serves 4-6.
NOTE: This salad will keep for several days. You can add pitted black olives, diced celery, or carrot strips.

CUCUMBERS IN SOUR CREAM

2 medium cucumbers	⅔ cup sour cream
1-2 teaspoons coarse salt	{ 1 tablespoon minced fresh dill *or* 1 teaspoon dill weed

Peel cucumbers with a vegetable peeler. Slice thin into a shallow bowl. Sprinkle each layer of cucumber slices with salt. Cover bowl and refrigerate for at least 1 hour. At serving time, drain off the water that has collected in the bowl. Add sour cream and dill. Serve in chilled glass bowls. Serves 4.

GROUND FLOOR SALAD

The Ground Floor is an "in" restaurant in New York with delicious food and austere elegance. There was nothing austere, however, about Monsieur Chevillot, the manager, who graciously shared the recipe for this special salad. Notice how little dressing is used in relation to the other ingredients. But don't change anything—this salad is superb.

3 cups endive	2 tablespoons olive oil
3 cups watercress	1 tablespoon red wine vinegar
1 cup sliced fresh mushrooms	1 teaspoon coarse salt
1½ cups sliced breast of turkey	½ teaspoon Dijon mustard
½ cup sliced ham	Freshly ground white pepper
¼ cup coarsely chopped walnuts	

Arrange the endive and watercress—which have been washed, dried, and crisped—in a large shallow salad bowl. Add the mushrooms, turkey, ham, and walnuts. In a small screw-top jar, measure the oil, vinegar, salt and mustard. Add freshly ground white pepper; cover and shake until blended. Add the dressing at the table, toss lightly, and serve immediately. Serves 3-4.

HAM SALAD

2 cups cubed cooked ham	½ cup sliced pitted black olives
½ cup diced celery	½ cup mayonnaise
½ cup diced green pepper	1 tablespoon red wine vinegar
¼ cup minced scallions	1 tablespoon cream or milk

Combine the ham, celery, green pepper, scallions, and olives in a medium bowl. Thin mayonnaise with vinegar and cream or milk and add. Taste to see if you need additional salt. Cover and chill until serving time. Serve on a bed of romaine with quartered tomatoes and hard cooked eggs. Serves 4.

LIME CREAM SALAD MOLD

This molded salad comes from my mother's file. It may seem a little old-fashioned now, but it does have a place in this collection. It is easy to make, can be done ahead of time, and tastes delicious.

1 package lime gelatin	1 cup diced cucumber
1½ cups boiling water	1 teaspoon Worcestershire sauce
1 cup sour cream	
1 can (8 ounces) crushed pineapple	

Dissolve gelatin in boiling water. Chill until mixture begins to thicken. Stir in sour cream, drained crushed pineapple, diced cucumber, and Worcestershire sauce. Pour into mold which has been rinsed in cold water or into individual ring molds. Chill until firm. Serves 4-5.

NOTE: This recipe can easily be doubled and turned into a ring mold. Fill the center with chunky lobster or chicken salad.

FRUIT SALAD MOLD

1 can (1 pound) pitted bing cherries	2 tablespoons (2 envelopes) unflavored gelatin
1 can (1 pound) boysenberries	1 tablespoon lemon juice
1 package (10 ounces) frozen raspberries, thawed	½ teaspoon salt
	½ cup coarsely chopped walnuts or almonds

Drain the cherries, boysenberries, and raspberries, reserving the juice. Soften the gelatin in ¼ cup of the juice. Heat ½ cup of the juice and stir into softened gelatin mixture until dissolved. Add lemon juice, salt, and remaining juice. Add fruit and nuts and turn into a ring mold which has been rinsed in cold water. Chill until firm. Serves 6-8.

SALADE NICOISE

Every restaurant, cafe, and brasserie along the French Riviera serves this salad, and no two are alike. I've tried to approximate the Niçoise I had for lunch one day at the Eden Roc in Cap d' Antibes. I don't know whether it was the exquisite setting, the view of the sparkling Mediterranean, or the general atmosphere, but it was an unforgettable meal.

6 cups shredded salad greens	3 tomatoes, quartered
½ cup vinaigrette dressing*	12 anchovies, drained
	12 pitted black olives
1 can (7 ounces) white tuna fish, drained	2 tablespoons capers
	1 tablespoon minced fresh parsley, dill, or tarragon
1 can (8 ounces) whole string beans, drained	

At serving time, arrange the salad greens in a large, shallow salad bowl. Toss with 3 or 4

*To make vinaigrette, measure 6 tablespoons of olive oil and 2 tablespoons of red or white wine vinegar into a screw-top jar. Add ½ teaspoon coarse salt, several turns of freshly ground pepper, and a crushed clove of garlic, if you like the flavor. Cover, shake, and chill.

tablespoons of the vinaigrette dressing. Arrange the tuna fish, string beans, tomatoes, anchovies, olives, and capers in mounds on the greens. Sprinkle with minced parsley, dill, or tarragon. Drizzle 3 or 4 more tablespoons of dressing over the salad, and toss again lightly. Serves 3-4.

PHILIP'S TROPICAL FRUIT SALAD

1 cup cubed apple
1 cup melon balls
1 cup sliced bananas
1 cup sliced
  strawberries
1 cup raisins, figs
  or dates
1½ cups sour cream

Combine apple, melon, bananas, and strawberries in a medium bowl. Any combination of fruit in season, except pineapple, may be used. Pour boiling water over the raisins, figs, or dates, let stand for a few seconds, then drain. Add to salad with sour cream. Mix thoroughly, cover, and chill until serving time. Sprinkle with ground nuts or shredded coconut. Serves 4-6.

SMOKED FISH SALAD

2 cups smoked fish*
2 hard-cooked eggs
½ cup chopped
  scallions

¼ cup mayonnaise
1 tablespoon lemon
  juice

Chop the fish with the eggs and scallions in a wooden bowl. Add mayonnaise and lemon juice. Extra seasoning is usually not required, but this depends on the fish. Serve as an appetizer spread on crisp stalks of celery, with buttered rye toast, or as a salad on Boston lettuce leaves with Greek olives and quartered tomatoes. Makes 2 cups.

*I use whitefish, Nova Scotia salmon, and even baked smoked salmon for this delicious salad. It can be made with leftover fresh cooked fish, too, but it needs to be pepped up with more seasoning.

HARRIET'S SPINACH SALAD

1 pound spinach
1 red onion
¼ cup packaged
  bacon-like bits
⅓ cup olive oil
1 tablespoon lemon
  juice

1 tablespoon wine
  vinegar
½ teaspoon coarse
  salt
4 turns freshly
  ground pepper

Use only young tender spinach for this salad. Wash the leaves thoroughly, dry them gently with paper towels, and crisp them in the refrigerator until serving time. Cut the onion into paper-thin slices and separate into rings. Sprinkle the bits over the salad and toss with remaining ingredients. Serves 4.

TOMATO SALAD

4 tomatoes
1 teaspoon minced fresh basil
3 tablespoons olive oil
1 tablespoon white wine vinegar
½ teaspoon coarse salt
Freshly ground black pepper

Wash, peel, and slice tomatoes into a shallow serving dish. (To peel tomatoes, cover them for a minute or two with boiling water. Spear each tomato at the blossom end with a fork and peel with paring knife.) Sprinkle the tomatoes with basil. In a small screw-top jar, combine oil, vinegar, salt, and pepper. Shake and drizzle over tomatoes. Cover and chill until serving time. Serves 4.

STUFFED TOMATOES

4 large tomatoes
1 cup pitted ripe olives
1 can (5 ounces) tiny shrimp, drained
½ cup chopped celery
3 tablespoons mayonnaise
1 tablespoon anchovy paste, if desired

Cover the tomatoes with boiling water and let stand for 2 minutes. Peel tomatoes, cut in half crosswise, scoop out some of the seed and pulp and invert on a plate to drain. Chop the olives, add the drained shrimp and celery. Mix mayonnaise with anchovy paste, if you like the taste, and combine with shrimp mixture. Pile into tomato halves. Serve on watercress. Serves 8.

WALDORF SALAD

3 apples	½ cup diced celery
3 tablespoons lemon juice	⅔ cup mayonnaise
1 tablespoon sugar	⅓ cup chopped pecans
Pinch of salt	

Core and dice the apples (use an apple slicer for a speedy job). Immediately sprinkle with lemon juice (to keep the apples from discoloring). Add sugar, salt, celery and mayonnaise; cover and chill. Add nuts just before serving. Serves 4-6.

JOAN'S CREAM DRESSING

Joan and I became friends when our children were small, and we were kitchen-bound. She is a rare combination—a born cook and a trained scientist—and she knows good food. I'm indebted to her for this—and many other recipes.

1 clove garlic, split
1 cup mayonnaise
1 tablespoon wine vinegar
1 tablespoon Worcestershire sauce
⅔ can anchovies with oil
1 tablespoon chopped parsley (fresh)
1 tablespoon chopped chives or scallions
Freshly ground pepper

Mix all ingredients in electric blender until blended. (Use all the oil from the anchovies.) NOTE: Use for tossed green salad. One word of caution—add at the very last minute, and use sparingly. The dressing is delicious, but heavy. A little goes a long way. Also, try it as a dip with crisp raw vegetables.

BASIC FRENCH DRESSING

6 tablespoons olive oil
2 tablespoons wine vinegar
½ teaspoon coarse salt
Freshly ground black pepper
1 clove garlic, minced or
1 large shallot, minced

Into a small screw-top jar pour the olive oil and vinegar. Add salt, pepper, garlic or shallot and shake.

SOUR CREAM FRENCH DRESSING

6 tablespoons olive
  oil
2 tablespoons white
  wine vinegar
¼ cup sour cream
½ teaspoon coarse
  salt
½ teaspoon sugar
¼ teaspoon paprika
  Grind of black
  pepper
1 clove garlic, split

Combine all the ingredients in a screw-top jar. Shake well and store in the refrigerator.

ROQUEFORT DRESSING I

½ cup sour cream
2 tablespoons (1
  ounce) crumbled
  Roquefort cheese
1 tablespoon white
  wine vinegar
¼ teaspoon coarse
  salt
¼ teaspoon prepared
  white horseradish
  Freshly ground
  pepper

Combine all ingredients in a screw-top jar. Chill until serving time. If dressing gets too thick, add a drop or two of milk or cream.

ROQUEFORT DRESSING II

½ cup olive oil
2 tablespoons red
  wine vinegar
2 tablespoons (1
  ounce) crumbled
  Roquefort cheese

2 tablespoons cream
  or milk
¼ teaspoon coarse
  salt
  Freshly ground
  black pepper

Combine all the ingredients in the blender at low speed. Pour into screw-top jar, cover, and chill until serving time.

SAUCES

Sauces are to cooking what accessories are to fashion. They make it possible to serve the same old thing and make it taste completely different.

We've already demonstrated several quick sauces at work. Prepared marinara sauce with a tomato or two and some discreet spices is delicious with chicken or veal. Canned chicken, beef, or mushroom gravy can be varied with wine, cream or cheese, and seasoning to enhance any number of meat, fish, or chicken dishes.

Here we look into some special sauces. With a blender, it's a cinch to make foolproof Hollandaise or Béarnaise sauce—even your own mayonnaise. Or with a good commercial brand of mayonnaise as a base, dozens of sauces can be made. Eleven suggestions are listed here.

Another base for delicious spreads is butter. You'll find seven here, but there are many more. To make them look pretty (without any dirty dishes), soften the butter on a large square of aluminum foil. Add the seasoning ingredients carefully. Shape the foil into a roll, twisting both ends tight. Chill until serving time, then open and cut the roll into round slices.

AVGOLEMONO SAUCE

3 egg yolks	½ teaspoon salt
4 teaspoons lemon juice	Dash of cayenne
	1 cup chicken stock
1 teaspoon arrow-root*	1 tablespoon finely minced parsley

In the top of a double boiler, mix the egg yolks with the lemon juice, arrowroot, salt, and cayenne. Beat lightly with a wire whisk, then slowly add the chicken stock while beating. Cook directly over moderate heat, stirring constantly, until sauce is thick enough to coat a silver spoon. (Don't let the sauce come anywhere near the boiling point, or you'll wind up with scrambled eggs.) Remove from heat and set over hot, not boiling, water, in the lower part of the double boiler; this will keep the sauce warm until you're ready to use it. Stir in the parsley just before serving. Serve with roast or charcoal-broiled lamb. Makes 1¼ cups.

*If arrowroot is not available, use 2 teaspoons of finely sifted flour.

BUTTER SAUCES

Anchovy Butter—To ½ cup (¼ pound) softened butter, add 1 tablespoon anchovy paste, ⅛ teaspoon salt and 2 teaspoons lemon juice. Serve with hot broiled fish or steak or as sandwich spread.

Chive Butter—To ½ cup softened butter, add 2 tablespoons finely minced chives and 2 teaspoons lemon juice. Serve with broiled meat or fish.

Curry Butter—To ½ cup softened butter, add ½ teaspoon curry powder and a dash of black pepper. Serve as sandwich spread, a base for fish canapés, or with hot vegetables, fish, or meat.

Garlic Butter—To ½ cup softened butter, add 2-3 crushed garlic cloves, a dash of salt and pepper, and ¼ teaspoon chopped parsley. Use for garlic bread, or on broiled meats.

Herb Butter—To ½ cup softened butter, add 2 tablespoons of minced chives, tarragon, chervil, dill, or a combination. Add a dash of salt and pepper. Serve over vegetables or broiled meat or fish.

Mustard Butter—To ½ cup softened butter, add ½ teaspoon dry mustard and a dash of salt and pepper. Serve with seafood or grilled meat or fish.

Tarragon Butter—To ½ cup softened butter, add 2 tablespoons minced fresh tarragon, 2 teaspoons lemon juice, and ¼ teaspoon coarse salt (if the butter is sweet). Serve with grilled steak or fish.

BLENDER HOLLANDAISE

I never could make good Hollandaise until the blender came along. Now I whip it up without a moment's hesitation for elegant asparagus or Eggs Benedict. The Béarnaise, given in the next recipe, is probably my favorite sauce of all; done in the blender, it works perfectly every time.

½ cup (¼ pound)   1 tablespoon lemon
  butter   juice
3 egg yolks   ¼ teaspoon salt
                         Dash of cayenne

Melt butter, but do not let it brown. Put egg yolks, lemon juice, salt, and cayenne into blender. Turn on low speed and add the hot butter in a steady stream. This should not take more than 15 seconds. Sauce will be smooth and slightly thickened. Makes ¾ cup.

BEARNAISE SAUCE

2 tablespoons white   1 tablespoon minced
  wine   fresh tarragon
2 tablespoons white   1 tablespoon minced
  wine vinegar   shallots

Combine ingredients in a small skillet and cook rapidly until almost all the liquid disappears. Cool and then beat the mixture into Blender Hollandaise (see preceding recipe) with a wire whisk or in the blender on high speed for 3 or 4 seconds. Serve with grilled steak or Fondue Bourguignonne (see page 111). Makes ¾ cup.

SAVORY HOT SAUCE

1 cup ketchup   sauce
1 tablespoon tarragon   2 drops Tabasco
  vinegar   sauce
1 tablespoon grated   Pinch of cayenne,
  onion   if desired
1 teaspoon
  Worcestershire

Combine ketchup, vinegar, onion, Worcestershire and Tabasco. For a very hot sauce, add cayenne. Chill. Serve with shellfish or Fondue Bourguignonne (see page 111). Makes 1 cup.

BLENDER MAYONNAISE

1 egg	¼ teaspoon dry
1 tablespoon lemon	mustard
juice*	1 cup oil (salad oil
¼ teaspoon salt	mixed with olive
	oil)

Put egg, lemon juice, salt, mustard, and ¼ cup of the oil into the blender. Cover and blend for 15 seconds at low speed. Remove cover, turn blender to high speed, and add remaining oil in a steady stream right into the center of the blender container.† (Do this as quickly as possible. And see that you're well covered—the mixture may spatter.) Makes 1 cup.

*1 tablespoon vinegar may be substituted for the lemon juice, but I prefer the taste of lemon in this dressing.
†If the mayonnaise thickens too quickly, add a few drops of lemon juice to change the consistency.

MAYONNAISE SAUCES

Aioli Sauce—To 1 cup mayonnaise, add 2 or 3 finely chopped or crushed garlic cloves. Serve as dip with vegetables or with meat or fish.
Avocado Mayonnaise—To 1 cup mayonnaise, add 1 mashed avocado and 1 teaspoon lemon juice. Serve with fruit salads or as a dip.
Caviar Sauce—To 1 cup mayonnaise, add 2

tablespoons black caviar and 1 teaspoon lemon juice. Serve as a dip or with sliced cold meat.

Chutney Sauce—To 1 cup mayonnaise, add ½ cup chopped chutney and 1 tablespoon lemon juice. Serve as dip or with hot or cold ham.

Dill Sauce—To 1 cup mayonnaise, add 1 tablespoon freshly minced dill, 1 teaspoon lemon juice, and some freshly ground black pepper. Serve as dip or with cucumbers, lettuce, or fish.

Horseradish Sauce—To 1 cup mayonnaise, add ¼ cup freshly grated horseradish or 2 tablespoons prepared white horseradish. Serve as dip or with cold meat or fish.

Mint Mayonnaise—To 1 cup mayonnaise, add 2 tablespoons chopped mint leaves and ½ teaspoon dry mustard. Serve with hot or cold lamb.

Orange Sauce—To 1 cup mayonnaise, add ¼ cup orange juice, 1 teaspoon grated orange rind and 1 teaspoon confectioners' sugar. Use with fresh fruit.

Roquefort Dressing—To 1 cup mayonnaise, add 2 tablespoons crumbled Roquefort cheese and ¼ cup whipped heavy cream or sour cream. Serve as dip or with tomatoes, green salad, cold meat, or fish.

Russian Dressing—To 1 cup mayonnaise, add ¼ cup chili sauce, 1 tablespoon cream or milk, 1 teaspoon lemon juice, and 2 tablespoons chopped sweet pickle. Serve as dip with vegetables, with cold shrimp, cold cuts, chicken, or green salad.

Tartar Sauce—To 1 cup mayonnaise, add 1 tablespoon capers, 1 tablespoon chopped sour pickle, 1 tablespoon finely chopped onion or chives, 1 tablespoon chopped parsley, and 1 teaspoon chopped tarragon. Serve as dip or with hot or cold fish.

MAYONNAISE VERTE

1 cup mayonnaise
¼ cup chopped
  scallions or chives
¼ cup chopped
  watercress
¼ cup chopped
  parsley
{ 1 tablespoon
  chopped fresh
  tarragon or
  1 teaspoon dried
  tarragon

{ 1 teaspoon fresh
  dill or
  ½ teaspoon dill weed
½ teaspoon chervil
1 tablespoon lemon
  juice

In a small bowl blend the mayonnaise with the chopped scallions, watercress, parsley, and tarragon. Add dill, chervil, and lemon juice and stir. Makes 1¼ cups.

NOTE: This sauce is traditionally served with poached salmon, but it is equally good with shrimp, lobster, crabmeat, and fresh fish. Try it, too, as a dip with raw vegetables.

PLUM (CHINESE DUK) SAUCE

1 cup plum jelly
½ cup chutney,
  chopped fine

1 tablespoon vinegar
2 teaspoons sugar

Combine all ingredients into a medium bowl. Beat with a fork until blended. Serve with spareribs, roast pork or as a dip for crisp Chinese noodles. Makes 1½ cups.

REMOULADE SAUCE

1 cup mayonnaise
1 tablespoon chopped capers
1 tablespoon chopped pickles
1 tablespoon chopped parsley
1 tablespoon chopped dill or tarragon
2 anchovy fillets, mashed

Combine the mayonnaise, drained capers, and pickles. Add parsley and dill or tarragon. Add mashed anchovies and chill. Serve with cold shellfish or Fondue Bourguignonne. (see page 111). Makes 1 cup.

DAVID'S SHALLOT SAUCE

3 tablespoons olive oil
2 tablespoons butter
¼ cup finely chopped shallots
½ cup chopped onion
½ teaspoon coarse salt
Freshly ground black pepper
¼ teaspoon Dijon mustard
1 teaspoon Worcestershire sauce
⅛ teaspoon paprika
¼ cup chicken stock

Heat olive oil and butter in a small saucepan. Add shallots and onion and cook until soft. Add salt, pepper, mustard, Worcestershire, and paprika. Stir in chicken stock and heat until bubbling. Serve sparingly with steak. Makes about ¾ cup.

SOUR CREAM-HORSERADISH SAUCE

1 cup sour cream
¼ cup grated fresh
   horseradish*
1 teaspoon sugar

¼ teaspoon coarse
   salt
Freshly ground
   pepper

Combine sour cream, horseradish, sugar, salt, and pepper. Marvelous with cold fish or meat. Makes 1 cup.

*If fresh horseradish is not available, use prepared white horseradish. Add slowly to sour cream and taste to determine how much you need.

QUICK TOMATO SAUCE

3 ripe tomatoes
¼ cup olive oil
2 cloves garlic,
   minced
1 tablespoon fresh
   basil leaves

1 tablespoon
   parsley
1 teaspoon coarse
   salt
Freshly ground
   black pepper

Peel the tomatoes and cut into the blender. Add oil, minced garlic, basil, parsley, salt, and pepper. Blend at low speed for 15 seconds. Heat and serve immediately with piping hot spaghetti, noodles, rice, green vegetables, or broiled fish. Makes 1¾ cups.

TUNA SAUCE

This is from the classic Vitello Tonnato in which a veal roast is cooked, chilled, and served with a tuna-caper sauce. The sauce is superb with cold veal, beef, or lamb. It is just as good as a dip with raw vegetables.

1 can (7 ounces) tuna fish in oil
1 teaspoon anchovy paste
¼ cup olive oil
½ cup chicken stock
1 tablespoon milk or cream
1 tablespoon lemon juice
1 tablespoon wine vinegar
2 tablespoons capers

Combine the tuna, anchovy paste, olive oil, chicken stock, milk or cream, lemon juice, and vinegar in the blender. Blend for 60 seconds at high speed. Add capers and serve with cold sliced meat.

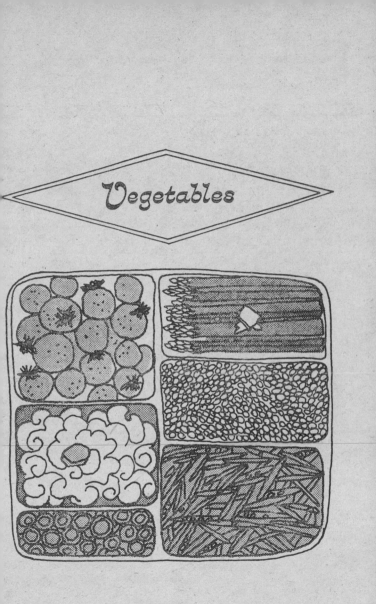

Vegetables

It's ironic that with all the abundance of our American markets and the ingenuity of canners and freezers, vegetables are neglected in our native cuisine. Good vegetable recipes are hard to find—cooks just don't seem interested in making them taste better.

The quickest way to improve the flavor of vegetables is to season them properly. Every cook knows the magic of a generous pat of butter, but there are other tricks. A dash of nutmeg in chopped spinach, a sprinkle of fresh dill in cooked carrots, a spoonful of cream does wonders for green peas. Another twist is to combine two vegetables such as squash and tomatoes, green peas and pearl onions, or mushrooms with string beans.

Most of the recipes in this section are based on canned vegetables. This was done in the interest of expedience—canned vegetables are already cooked, and merely require heating. You will also want to try some of the frozen vegetables that, heated in their plastic pouches, are almost as quick to prepare. And when young asparagus tips or tender string beans are available at your supermarket, you'll surely want to take advantage of their freshness. Fresh or frozen vegetables can be used in any recipe here.

ASPARAGUS WITH LEMON BUTTER SAUCE

This is a good quick sauce to serve with many vegetables. We use it with cauliflower, broccoli, and French-style green beans.

1 can (1 pound) asparagus
¼ cup butter
2 tablespoons lemon juice

2 tablespoons flavored bread crumbs
¼ teaspoon coarse salt
Freshly ground black pepper

Heat asparagus in liquid. At serving time, drain the asparagus and arrange in shallow serving dish. Melt butter in the same skillet, add lemon juice, bread crumbs, salt, and pepper. Pour hot sauce over asparagus and serve immediately. Serves 3-4.

ZESTY BAKED BEANS

2 cans (1 pound each) baked beans
½ cup chopped onion
1 clove garlic, crushed

1-2 tablespoons soy sauce
1-2 tablespoons bourbon

Turn the beans into a medium oven-proof casserole. Add onion, garlic, soy sauce, and bourbon. Heat in a moderate (350 degree) oven for 30 minutes or until piping hot and bubbling. Serves 6-8.

GREEN BEAN CASSEROLE

This recipe has been around for years, but it's quick as a wink, and somehow it tastes like an elegant party dish.

2 cans (1 pound each) French-style green beans	1 teaspoon soy sauce
	¼ teaspoon salt
1 can (10½ ounces) cream of mush-room soup	1 can (3½ ounces) French fried onion rings

Drain the beans and turn into a medium oven-proof quart casserole. Add soup (undiluted), soy sauce, salt, and half of the French fried onions, and toss lightly to combine. Sprinkle the rest of the onions over the top. Heat in a moderate (350 degree) oven until onions are crisp and the sauce is bubbling. Serves 6.

GREEN BEAN MELANGE

1 can (1 pound) blue lake green beans, drained	½ teaspoon coarse salt
1 can (8 ounces) whole tomatoes	¼ teaspoon oregano Freshly ground black pepper
1 can (8 ounces) tiny whole onions, drained	

Into a medium saucepan, turn the drained beans, the tomatoes with their liquid, and the drained onions. Add salt, oregano, and pepper and heat until bubbling. Serves 4.

GREEN BEANS WITH MUSHROOMS

2 tablespoons butter
1 can (2 ounces) sliced mushrooms, drained

1 can (1 pound) French-style green beans, drained
Sprig of tarragon

Melt the butter in a saucepan; add the sliced mushrooms and sauté for a minute or two. Add the beans, toss lightly, and heat. Add tarragon, minced. Serves 3-4.

LIMA BEANS AU GRATIN

This is another quick ploy for dressing up vegetables. Shred some cheese in your Mouli grater, melt quickly over the hot vegetable, add soy sauce for zest, and be prepared to serve seconds.

1 can (1 pound) baby lima beans
½ teaspoon soy sauce

½ cup shredded sharp cheddar cheese

Into a medium saucepan turn the baby lima beans with liquid. Heat thoroughly. A few minutes before serving, drain carefully. Add the soy sauce and shredded cheese. Stir over low heat until cheese melts. Serves 3-4.

LIMA BEANS WITH WATER CHESTNUTS

1 can (1 pound) baby lima beans	½ teaspoon coarse salt
1 can (5 ounces) water chestnuts	Freshly ground black pepper
2 tablespoons butter	1 tablespoon finely minced parsley
1 teaspoon red wine vinegar	

Into a medium saucepan turn the lima beans and liquid. Slice the water chestnuts and add. Heat until bubbling. Just before serving, drain completely. Add butter, vinegar, salt, and pepper. Heat until butter melts. Turn into serving dish and sprinkle with parsley. Serves 4.

BRAISED ENDIVE

4 stalks endive	½ teaspoon coarse salt
½ cup chicken broth	
1 tablespoon butter	1 turn of freshly ground pepper

Place endive and chicken broth, with butter, salt and pepper in saucepan. Cover, bring to a boil and simmer for 10 minutes. Serves 2.

CHINESE CABBAGE

1 small head green
   cabbage
¼ cup butter
1 teaspoon coarse
   salt
   Freshly ground
   black pepper
2 teaspoons soy
   sauce
1 tablespoon lemon
   juice

Remove the tough outer leaves of the cabbage. Wash, core and shred finely. In a large skillet, melt the butter. Add the shredded cabbage with salt, pepper, soy sauce, and lemon juice. Cover and cook until tender. (If you like it crunchy, cook only for 7 minutes.) Serves 4-6.

RED CABBAGE WITH APPLE

1 jar (1 pound) sweet
   and sour red cabbage
1 apple, cored and
   cubed

Heat the red cabbage with cubed apple until bubbling. Serves 4-6.

CARROTS WITH GRAPES

1 can (1 pound) cooked carrots	¼ teaspoon garlic salt
1 can (8 ounces) seedless grapes	4 basil leaves or ½ teaspoon dried basil
2 tablespoons butter	
2 tablespoons lemon juice	

Into a saucepan put the drained carrots and grapes. Add butter, lemon, garlic salt, and shredded basil leaves. Heat thoroughly. Serves 4.

CARROT TSIMMIS

This is a perfect recipe. It's a quick and delicious version of a Jewish dish that traditionally took hours to make.

1 can (1 pound) sliced carrots, drained	drained
	⅓ cup butter
1 can (18 ounces) sweet potatoes,	¾ cup maple-flavored syrup

Arrange a layer of carrot slices in a medium oven-proof casserole. Cover with a layer of cut sweet potatoes. Dot with butter. Alternate carrots and sweet potatoes; dot each layer with butter. Pour syrup over the top. Bake in a moderate (350 degree) oven for 90 minutes, or until syrup is absorbed. Serves 4-6.

SALLY'S CAULIFLOWER AU GRATIN

A friend found this method of cooking fro-
zen cauliflower in a government booklet. I was
very skeptical about it but found that it works
perfectly and tastes delicious.

2 packages (10   ½ cup milk
   ounces each)   ½ cup shredded sharp
   frozen cauliflower   cheddar cheese
1 cup boiling water   2 tablespoons
1 can (10½ ounces)   flavored bread
   cream of mushroom   crumbs
   soup   1 tablespoon butter

Arrange the cauliflower in a medium oven-
proof casserole. Pour boiling water over the
cauliflower and set into a moderate (350 degree) oven for 10 minutes. In the meantime,
turn the soup into a small bowl. Add milk and
cheese, and stir to combine. When the 10 minutes are up, drain the water from the casserole,
and pour the soup-cheese mixture over the
cauliflower. Sprinkle flavored bread crumbs
over the top, and dot with butter. Return to
oven, and heat for about 40 minutes, or until
cauliflower is tender. Serves 5-6.

COLORFUL CORN

2 tablespoons butter
½ cup cubed cooked
  ham
½ cup chopped onion
½ cup chopped green
  pepper
¼ cup chopped
  pimiento

1 can (1 pound)
whole kernel corn,
drained
½ teaspoon coarse
salt
Freshly ground
black pepper

In a medium skillet, melt the butter. Add the cubed ham, chopped onion and green pepper and sauté until soft. Add pimiento and drained corn, salt, and pepper. Mix lightly and heat until piping hot. Serves 4-5.

SOUTHERN OKRA

2 tablespoons butter
½ cup chopped onion
1 can (1 pound) cut
  okra, well drained
1 can (8 ounces)
  peeled tomatoes,
  drained

¼ teaspoon coarse
salt
Freshly ground
black pepper

In a medium saucepan, melt the butter. Add chopped onion and cook for a minute or two until soft. Add drained okra and tomatoes and heat until bubbling. Add salt and pepper and serve immediately. Serves 4.

ONIONS WITH NUTS

2 tablespoons butter
¼ cup pignolia nuts
1 can (1 pound)
   tiny whole onions,
drained
Dash of coarse
   salt

Melt the butter in a medium saucepan. Add the nuts and shake until they turn yellow. Add the drained onions and a dash of salt. Heat onions through. Serves 3-4.

FRENCH-STYLE GREEN PEAS

This is my favorite green pea recipe. For a minimum of fuss you get a maximum effect.

4-5 leaves Boston
   lettuce, washed
1 package (10
   ounces) frozen
   green peas
2 tablespoons
chopped onion
1 tablespoon butter
¼ teaspoon salt
Freshly ground
   pepper
2 tablespoons heavy
   cream

Line a medium skillet (which has a tight-fitting cover) with the leaves of Boston lettuce. Add frozen green peas, onion, butter, salt, and pepper. Cover tightly and cook over very low heat for 5 or 6 minutes. Separate the peas with a fork. Cover again and cook until peas are thawed. Continue to cook until peas are cooked

through. Add heavy cream, stir, and heat.
Serves 4.

GREEN PEAS WITH DILL

1 can (1 pound)
  tiny green peas
1 tablespoon butter
¼ cup sour cream

{ 2 tablespoons
  minced fresh dill *or*
 1 teaspoon dill weed
¼ teaspoon coarse
  salt

Heat peas in their liquid. Just before serving, drain and add butter, sour cream, dill and salt. Heat again, but do not boil. Serves 3-4.

MINTED PEAS

1 can (1 pound) green
  peas
2 tablespoons butter
1 tablespoon lemon
  juice

1 tablespoon finely
  chopped mint
Dash of salt

Heat peas in their liquid. Just before serving, drain the peas. Add butter, lemon juice, and mint. Add salt if necessary. Heat again until piping hot. Serves 3-4.

POTATOES IN CREAM

1 can (1 pound)
  peeled white
  potatoes
1 can (8 ounces)
  tiny whole onions

¼ cup sour cream
1 tablespoon
  chopped chives

Turn the potatoes and onions (with some of the liquid) in a medium saucepan. Heat until piping hot. Just before serving, drain the liquid. Add the sour cream and chives, mix gently, and reheat, but do not boil. Serves 4.

HOT POTATO SALAD

1 can (1 pound)
  sliced white
  potatoes
¼ cup chopped onion
¼ cup chopped green
  pepper
¼ cup white wine
  vinegar

1 tablespoon water
1 teaspoon coarse
  salt
1 teaspoon sugar
4 turns freshly
  ground pepper
¼ cup salad (not
  olive) oil

Drain the potatoes. Turn them into a medium bowl with onion and green pepper. Heat vinegar, water, salt, sugar, and pepper in a small saucepan until it reaches the boiling point. Pour over potatoes with salad oil. Toss lightly so potatoes won't break. Serve hot or cold. Serves 3-4.

SCALLOPED POTATOES

1 can (1 pound) sliced white potatoes, drained	1 tablespoon flour
	2 tablespoons butter
¼ cup chopped onion	½ teaspoon coarse salt
½ cup freshly grated cheese (cheddar or Parmesan)	Freshly ground pepper
	½ cup milk

Arrange one layer of sliced potatoes in a small oven-proof casserole. Sprinkle with chopped onion, grated cheese, and flour. Dot with butter. Alternate layers of potatoes with chopped onion, cheese, flour, and butter. Finish with a layer of cheese. Sprinkle with salt and pepper. Pour the milk over all. Heat in a moderate (350 degree) oven for 30 minutes or until piping hot. Serves 3-4.

HOLIDAY SWEET POTATOES

When I first tasted this, one Thanksgiving many years ago, it was made with marshmallows. I've served it many times since then—sometimes with and other times without marshmallows. I think it's more unusual without the marshmallows, but here is the recipe the way it was given to me.

2 cans (1 pound each) sweet potatoes, drained
1 can (8 ounces) crushed pineapple, drained

½ cup pecans
¼ cup brown sugar
¼ cup butter
½ cup honey
8 marshmallows, if desired

Arrange the sweet potatoes in a buttered shallow oven-proof casserole. Sprinkle the drained crushed pineapple over the sweet potatoes. Sprinkle with pecans, then brown sugar. Dot with butter. Drizzle honey over all. If you want to use marshmallows, quarter them and arrange over the top. Heat in a moderate (350 degree) oven until bubbling, about 20 minutes. Serves 6.

SWEET POTATO SUPREME

1 can (1 pound) sweet potatoes
2 tablespoons butter
1 tablespoon Cointreau

¼ teaspoon coarse salt
Freshly ground black pepper

Heat sweet potatoes in their liquid until piping hot. Just before serving, drain the potatoes. Mash with fork or ricer and add butter, Cointreau, salt, and pepper. Serve immediately. Serves 3-4.

DILLED SAUERKRAUT

*For sauerkraut fans, this is a must. When I
serve roast loin of pork, I make Dilled Sauerkraut and heat it in the roasting pan with the
pork.*

1 can (1 pound) sauerkraut	1 red apple
2 tablespoons butter	1 teaspoon dill weed
½ cup chopped onion	2 tablespoons brown sugar

Drain sauerkraut completely. In a medium
skillet melt the butter. Add chopped onion and
the apple which has been cored and cubed (but
not peeled). Add sauerkraut, dill weed, and
brown sugar. Mix thoroughly and cook until
piping hot. Serves 4-5.

SAVORY SPINACH

1 pound fresh spinach	1 teaspoon coarse salt
2 tablespoons olive oil	1 clove garlic, minced
	2 tablespoons butter

Wash the spinach thoroughly; remove the
stems. In a large skillet, heat the oil with salt
and minced garlic. Add the spinach and sauté
for 2-3 minutes, stirring constantly. Add the
butter, cover, and cook for about 3 minutes.
Serves 3-4.

SQUASH WITH PEANUTS

1 can (1 pound) yellow squash*
½ cup heavy cream
2 tablespoons grated onion
2 tablespoons butter
1 teaspoon coarse salt
Freshly ground black pepper
½ cup salted peanuts

In a medium bowl, mix the squash with cream, onion, butter, salt, and pepper. Spoon into a buttered shallow baking dish or pie plate. Heat in a moderate (350 degree) oven for 45 minutes or until piping hot. Sprinkle with toasted salted peanuts. Serves 4-6.
*If you can't find canned squash, use frozen or fresh-cooked squash. Or try this dish with pumpkin—add a dash of nutmeg and cinnamon.

GRILLED TOMATOES

3 medium tomatoes
2 tablespoons butter
1 tablespoon flour
1 teaspoon coarse salt
¼ teaspoon dried basil

Cut tomatoes into thick slices. Spread each slice with butter and arrange in one layer in a shallow baking dish. Mix flour with salt and basil and sprinkle over tomato slices. Place under the broiler, about 3 inches from the heat, for 5 minutes. Serves 4.

ZUCCHINI BAKE

1 can (1 pound)
    Italian-style
    zucchini
½ cup sliced pitted
    ripe olives
1 can (2 ounces)
    sliced mushrooms,
    drained

2 tablespoons
    chopped shallots
    or onion
¼ teaspoon oregano
½ cup freshly grated
    Parmesan cheese

Turn the zucchini with liquid into a medium oven-proof casserole. Add olives, drained mushrooms, shallots or onion, and oregano. Sprinkle cheese over the top. Heat in a moderate (350 degree) oven about 20 minutes, or until it is piping hot and the cheese has melted. Serves 4-5.

Rice

When I was going through the various categories of quick recipes for this book, my husband made a valuable suggestion: Why not buy a pint of cooked rice from the local Chinese restaurant and experiment with it at home?

It seemed like a great idea for a hurry-up dish, and I decided to try it. For less than a quarter I bought a pint of perfectly cooked, fluffy white rice. And in a matter of minutes I transformed it into a gourmet Rice Trieste.

Ever since that first successful experiment, I've been buying cooked rice. My husband gently reminded me the other day that I used to cook my own. But the Chinese rice is so convenient and delicious that I'm afraid I'm hooked.

Rice is also available in cans. The Spanish rice is quite good, and I have used it in another section with shrimp. Canned wild rice, which is excellent, is also included in a Turkey and Wild Rice recipe. The reason I haven't used canned wild rice more often is that it's not readily available.

There are also several brands of quick-cooking processed rice that can be substituted for any of the above.

FRIEDA'S RICE WITH ARTICHOKES

Frieda adapted this recipe from the rice salad served and sold at the Old Denmark shop in New York. It is very rich, but a superb dish. Serve it as an appetizer, a salad with cold sliced meat, or with hot soup for a perfect supper.

2 cups (1 pint) cooked white rice
1 can (9 ounces) artichoke hearts, drained
6 tablespoons olive oil
2 tablespoons red wine vinegar
1 tablespoon lemon juice
1 teaspoon coarse salt
Freshly ground black pepper
¼ teaspoon sweet paprika
½ cup mayonnaise
2 tablespoons heavy cream
2 tablespoons (1 ounce) Roquefort cheese, crumbled
2 tablespoons diced pimiento
2 tablespoons minced parsley
1 tablespoon minced dill

Turn the rice into a strainer. Run hot water through it and drain. Turn into a medium bowl. Add drained artichoke hearts, oil, vinegar, lemon, salt, pepper, and paprika, and toss gently. Cover and chill until serving time. Just before serving, mix mayonnaise with heavy cream and 1 tablespoon of the Roquefort cheese until smooth. Add the remaining tablespoon of Roquefort to the mayonnaise with pimiento, parsley, and dill. Add to rice and artichoke dish, toss lightly, and serve on Boston lettuce. Serves 4-6.

RED BEANS WITH RICE

2 cups (1 pint)
    cooked rice
2 tablespoons olive
    oil
¼ cup chopped onion
¼ cup chopped green
    pepper
1 clove garlic,
    minced
1 teaspoon coarse
    salt
Freshly ground
    black pepper
1 can (1 pound) red
    kidney beans
Parsley, minced

Turn the rice into a strainer. Run hot water through the rice and drain. In a medium skillet heat the olive oil with the onion, green pepper, and garlic. Add salt and pepper. Drain beans, add to the skillet and heat. Add rice, mix, and heat through. Top with freshly minced parsley. Serves 4.

SUSAN'S COLD CURRIED RICE

Susan is my career-girl stepdaughter, and a great cook in her own right. She serves this dish with a green salad and hot rolls, and everyone adores it.

2 cups (1 pint) cooked
    white rice
1 cup (5 ounces)
    frozen cooked
    shrimp, defrosted
3 tablespoons
    mayonnaise
2 tablespoons lemon
    juice
1 teaspoon curry
    powder
1 teaspoon coarse
    salt
Freshly ground
    black pepper
1 teaspoon grated
    onion

In a medium salad bowl combine rice, shrimp, mayonnaise, lemon juice, curry powder, salt, pepper, and grated onion. Cover and chill until serving time. Serves 4-5.

NOTE: This makes a mild curry. If you like it hotter, add more curry powder, but do it a little bit at a time.

HOPPIN' JOHN

This is a dish with a history. It is traditionally served in the South on New Year's Day, and is supposed to bring good luck. I don't think it's a dish for every taste, but it's easy to make and different enough to be worth trying.

2 tablespoons olive oil
½ cup chopped onion
1 cup diced cooked ham
1 can (15 ounces) blackeye peas, drained

2 cups (1 pint) cooked white rice
1 teaspoon coarse salt
Freshly ground black pepper
Dash of Tabasco sauce
¼ cup packaged bacon-like bits

Heat the olive oil in a medium skillet. Add onion and ham, and sauté for 1 to 2 minutes. Add drained blackeye peas, rice, salt, pepper, and Tabasco. Cook until piping hot. Turn into shallow serving dish. Sprinkle with bits. Serves 4.

RICE AL PESTO

If you like the taste of garlic, you'll love this great Italian dish. The sauce is made in the blender, and it's just as good with spaghetti, meat, chicken, fish, or as a dip with raw vegetables.

2 cups (1 pint) cooked white rice
½ cup olive oil
2 cloves garlic, sliced
¼ cup pignolia nuts
¼ cup freshly grated Parmesan cheese
2 tablespoons parsley
2 tablespoons fresh basil leaves *or*
¼ teaspoon dried basil
½ teaspoon coarse salt

Keep the rice hot by steaming over boiling water while preparing sauce. Turn oil, garlic, nuts, cheese, parsley, fresh or dried basil, and salt into blender. Blend at high speed for 15 seconds. Toss lightly with hot rice and serve immediately. Serves 4.

QUICK RICE PUDDING

2 cups (1 pint) cooked white rice
1 cup heavy cream, whipped
¼ cup sugar
1 teaspoon vanilla
¼ teaspoon ground cinnamon
Dash of nutmeg
⅔ cup (2 individual packages) raisins, plumped*

Combine the rice, whipped cream, sugar, vanilla, cinnamon, and nutmeg. Stir in raisins, cover, and chill. Serves 4-6.

*To plump the raisins, pour boiling water over them. Let stand a minute or two, then drain.

GLORIA'S SCALLION RICE

Since this recipe calls for only the green part of the scallion, it requires 3 bunches of scallions. Try it this way, and then with the whole scallion (1 bunch should do it). It's stronger with the whole scallion, but excellent either way. Use the sauce for noodles, too.

½ cup (1 stick) butter	1 teaspoon coarse salt
2 cups minced scallions	2 cups (1 pint) cooked white rice

Melt the butter over very low heat. Add scallion greens and sauté until soft. Add salt and stir in rice. Heat through and serve. Serves 4.

SPECIAL SEAFOOD CASSEROLE

3 cups seafood*
¼ cup chopped onion
¼ cup chopped green pepper
¼ cup chopped pimiento
1½ cups cooked rice
½ cup mayonnaise
½ cup sandwich spread
2 tablespoons cream or milk
2 teaspoons Worcestershire sauce
1 teaspoon lemon juice
½ teaspoon salt
Freshly ground pepper
Freshly grated Parmesan cheese

Mix seafood with onion, pepper, pimiento, and rice. Add mayonnaise, sandwich spread, cream, Worcestershire, lemon, salt, and pepper. Turn into medium oven-proof casserole; top with Parmesan. Heat in a moderate (350 degree) oven until bubbling. Serves 4-6.

*My favorite combination is 1 cup shrimp (cooked, of course), 1 cup crabmeat, and 1 cup lobster, but any combination of fresh, canned, or frozen seafood will do.

SPINACH RICE

2 eggs, well beaten
½ cup cream or milk
2 cups grated sharp
  cheddar cheese
  (about ½ pound)
¼ cup butter,
  softened
1 can (8 ounces)
  chopped spinach,
  well drained

1 tablespoon grated
  onion
1 teaspoon Worces-
  tershire sauce
½ teaspoon coarse
  salt
¼ teaspoon dried
  thyme
2 cups (1 pint)
  cooked white rice

In a buttered oven-proof casserole, combine the beaten eggs, cream or milk, 1½ cups of the grated cheese, butter, and well-drained spinach. Add onion, Worcestershire, salt, thyme, and rice. Mix lightly. Sprinkle remaining cheese over the top. Heat in a moderate (350 degree) oven for 30 to 40 minutes or until firm. Serves 4-6.

RICE TRIESTE

We were served rice with clam sauce at a fabulous Northern Italian restaurant in New York called Giordano's. I think the version we made at home is just as good. Of course this quick sauce is perfect for spaghetti, too.

1 can (10½ ounces)
  white clam sauce
1 clove garlic,
  minced
¼ teaspoon oregano
2 cups (1 pint)
  cooked white rice

1 teaspoon salt
  Freshly ground
  black pepper
2 tablespoons freshly
  grated Parmesan
  cheese

In a medium saucepan, heat the white clam sauce with garlic and oregano. Turn the rice into a strainer. Run hot water through the rice and shake to drain. When the sauce is bubbling, add the rice, salt, and pepper. Heat until piping hot. Turn into a serving dish; sprinkle freshly grated Parmesan cheese over the top. Serve immediately. Serves 4.

Quick Desserts

Dessert adds a final fillip to a good meal. It need not be elaborate—sometimes the simplest dessert is the most elegant—but a taste of sweetness to satisfy the soul.

Instant dessert seems to be the preoccupation of every food manufacturer in the country. There are instant puddings, custards, cake mixes, pie fillings and crusts, fruit in jars, cans, and freezer containers—the list could go on and on. Some of these products are excellent; others, like synthetic whipped cream, are appalling. The trick is to try them all, and select the ones that not only save time but taste good.

Fruit is a wonderful dessert. Fresh strawberries with Kirsch, canned orange sections with cocoanut, sautéed bananas in orange juice and rum are perfect desserts. Fruit and cheese were made to go together, as the Europeans know.

Ice cream is another favorite standby. With fruit, cake, or cookies, it manages to be simple and gala at the same time. Read on for some specific suggestions for finishing your meals on a note of triumph.

APPLE CHARLOTTE

1 package (12) lady-
  fingers
2 tablespoons Kirsch
1 jar (20 ounces)
  chunky applesauce*

1 can (1 pound)
  French vanilla
  pudding

Split the ladyfingers and arrange a layer of
halves in the bottom of a small soufflé dish or
serving bowl. Sprinkle 1 tablespoon of the
Kirsch over the ladyfingers. Spread a layer of
chunky applesauce over the ladyfingers. Then
spread a thin layer of French vanilla pudding.
Follow with another layer of ladyfingers; sprinkle with remaining Kirsch. Add another layer
of applesauce and vanilla pudding. If there are
any ladyfingers left, use them to decorate the
top. Cover and chill until serving time. Serves
6-8.
*You may vary this dessert by using some of the
combinations available—apples with strawberries,
raspberries, or apricots.

APRICOT BAVARIAN CREAM

1 package lemon
  gelatin
1½ cups boiling
  water
2 jars (4 ounces
  each) puréed
  apricots*

½ cup heavy cream,
  whipped
1 tablespoon
  brandy, if
  desired

Dissolve gelatin in boiling water. Chill until mixture begins to thicken. Add apricot purée. Fold in whipped cream and brandy. Pour into mold which has been rinsed in cold water. Chill until firm. Serves 4-5.

*You can substitute 1 can (8 ounces) apricots—drained, pitted, and puréed in the blender—for the baby-style apricots. Or you can use 1 cup of apricot nectar, and reduce the amount of boiling water to 1 cup.

HATTIE'S GLAZED BANANAS

4 bananas	¼ cup orange juice
½ cup (¼ pound) butter	¼ cup honey
	1-2 tablespoons rum

Peel bananas and cut in half lengthwise. Melt half the butter in a shallow saucepan. Sauté bananas, turning until very lightly browned. Remove bananas, add remaining butter, orange juice, honey, and rum. Stir and cook for a few minutes until thick. Add bananas and heat until piping hot and thoroughly glazed. Serve at once, alone or with ice cream. Serves 4.

CHOCOLATE WAFER ROLL

19 thin chocolate wafers	1 teaspoon sugar
1 cup heavy cream, whipped	½ teaspoon vanilla
	½ teaspoon almond flavoring

Spread the chocolate wafers generously with sweetened, flavored whipped cream. Arrange the wafers on edge on a rectangular serving platter, reserving one wafer to use as a garnish. Frost the top and sides of the log with remaining cream. Crush the remaining wafer and sprinkle the crumbs over the top. Cover with plastic wrap and chill for 2 hours or more. Cut in diagonal slices. Serves 4-5.

NOTE: If you're in a hurry, chill the roll in the freezing compartment of your refrigerator. Thirty minutes should do it.

COFFEE TOFFEE TART

6 individual sponge shells	1 tablespoon (1 envelope) pre-melted chocolate
2 tablespoons crème de cacao, if desired	2½ teaspoons instant coffee powder
½ cup (¼ pound) butter, softened	2 eggs
½ cup confectioners' sugar	½ cup heavy cream
	1 tablespoon confectioners' sugar

Arrange the sponge shells on a flat plate; sprinkle 1 teaspoon crème de cacao over each. With portable electric beater, cream butter. Add ½ cup confectioners' sugar and continue to beat until fluffy. Add melted chocolate and 2 teaspoons of the instant coffee. Add 1 egg and beat until light. Add second egg; beat 5 minutes more. Turn into sponge shells (you may have some left over). Cover and chill until firm—at least 2 hours. At serving time, whip heavy cream; add ½ teaspoon instant coffee and 1 tablespoon confectioners' sugar and blend thoroughly. Top each shell with a generous dollop of cream. Serves 6.

GINGERED FIGS

1 can (1 pound)   ½ cup coarsely
   kadota figs   chopped walnuts
½ cup ginger
   marmalade

Drain figs, but reserve the liquid. Add the marmalade to the liquid and stir until combined. Chill the figs in the ginger liquid until serving time. Add about 2 tablespoons of the coarsely chopped walnuts to each serving of figs and juice. Serves 4.

FRUIT BAVARIAN CREAM

1 package   1 package (10
   strawberry gelatin   ounces) frozen
1½ cups hot water   strawberries,
1 pint vanilla ice   thawed
   cream

Dissolve the gelatin in the hot water. Add ice cream and chill until thickened. Add thawed and drained strawberries. Turn into a mold which has been rinsed in cold water. Chill until firm. Serves 4-5.

NOTE: This molded dessert can be made with lemon, cherry, or pineapple gelatin. Raspberries, blueberries, or mixed frozen fruit can be substituted for the strawberries.

GRAHAM APPLE PUDDING

12 graham crackers
1 jar (20 ounces)
   applesauce
1 cup heavy cream

2-3 tablespoons
    confectioners'
    sugar
1 tablespoon
    curaçao

Arrange 4 of the graham crackers on a serving plate. Cover with one-third of the applesauce. Cover with another layer of 4 crackers and another third of the applesauce. Top with remaining crackers and applesauce. Whip cream with sugar until stiff; add curaçao. Frost sides and top of cracker mixture and put in freezer until firm. Serves 6.

GRAPE SURPRISE

3 cups seedless green
  grapes
⅓ cup sour cream

3 tablespoons
  granulated brown
  sugar
2 tablespoons crème
  de cacao, if desired

Wash and stem the grapes. Add sour cream and combine. Sprinkle brown sugar over the fruit, and taste for desired sweetness. Cover and chill until serving time. Add the crème de cacao just before serving—it will transform a really good dessert into a festive company treat. Serves 4-6.

QUICK CHOCOLATE MOUSSE

My husband still talks about the night he tasted eight chocolate mousses. This was the quickest and the best. One word of caution, though. It won't work well if you try to chill the mousse in a mold. But it works perfectly in individual coupes.

1 tablespoon (1 envelope) unflavored gelatin
¼ cup cold water
½ cup hot coffee
1 package (6 ounces) semisweet chocolate bits
1 tablespoon sugar
2 egg yolks
1 cup heavy cream
1 tablespoon curaçao
1 heaping cup crushed ice
1 package (12) ladyfingers

Put gelatin, water, and hot coffee into blender. Blend on high speed for 1 minute. Add chocolate bits and sugar. Blend on high speed for 10 seconds or until chocolate is blended. Add yolks, cream, curaçao, and ice. Blend on high speed for 20 seconds. Split the ladyfingers and stand them up in 8 coupe glasses. Pour the mousse into the coupes. Chill for several hours or until set. Serves 8.

LEMON SYLLABUB

1 lemon
⅓ cup dry white wine
1½ cups heavy cream
4 tablespoons sugar

Grate the rind of the lemon, then squeeze the juice into a small dish. Add the rind and the wine. Whip the cream until it holds its shape, then beat in the lemon mixture and the sugar. Pile into parfait or coupe glasses and chill 2 to 3 hours in refrigerator. Serve with cookies or plain cake. Serves 4-5.

ORANGE CREAM CAKE

I've been making this cake for special occasions for years, yet every time I soak the layers with the orange juice mixture, I'm convinced I've made a mistake. Don't worry—the cake absorbs the liquid without falling apart. And when it's thoroughly chilled and frosted with the cream, the cake is moist and absolutely delicious.

1 9-inch sponge cake	1 tablespoon
2 eggs, separated	Cointreau
½ cup orange juice	1 cup heavy cream,
½ teaspoon grated	whipped
orange rind	1 teaspoon
⅓ cup sugar	confectioners'
	sugar

Split sponge cake into 2 layers with a serrated knife. Place each layer on a large, flat plate. Beat egg whites until stiff, but not dry. Add yolks and continue beating. Add orange juice, rind, and sugar, beating all the time. Add Cointreau. Pour the orange juice mixture over the two layers. Cover with plastic wrap and refrigerate for at least 3 hours, preferably overnight. At serving time, place one layer on a cake plate. Cover with whipped cream which has been mixed with confectioners' sugar. Place second layer on top and cover with whipped cream. Serves 6.

PAULINE'S ORANGE SHERBET MOLD

1 package orange gelatin
1 cup boiling water
1 can (11 ounces) mandarin orange sections
1 pint orange sherbet, softened
1 tablespoon curaçao, if desired

Dissolve gelatin in boiling water. Add ½ cup liquid from the mandarin orange sections. Chill until mixture begins to thicken. Stir in the softened sherbet, the drained orange sections, and the curaçao. Pour into mold which has been rinsed in cold water. Chill until firm. Serves 4-5.

SURPRISE CAKE

It's a strange thing about recipes. During a lifetime of cooking, I had never heard of a dessert made with pound cake and sour cream. Then I ran across two recipes within forty-eight hours, and from entirely different sources. This recipe and the one following are both excellent, and worth a try.

4 slices pound cake
1 cup sour cream
¼ cup granulated brown sugar
¼ cup slivered blanched almonds

Spread one side of each slice of pound cake with sour cream. Sprinkle about 1 teaspoon of brown sugar over the sour cream, and arrange the slice of cake carefully, spread side down in a serving dish. Spread the other side and all the edges with sour cream. Sprinkle with about 2 teaspoons of brown sugar and 1 tablespoon of slivered almonds. Repeat for each slice of cake. Carefully cover the dish with plastic wrap and chill for at least 3 hours, preferably longer. Serves 4.

SEVEN LAYER SURPRISE CAKE

1 frozen pound cake   1 package (6 ounces)
  (12 ounces)   milk chocolate bits
1 cup sour cream   ¼ cup hot coffee

Let the cake thaw enough to slice. Turn the cake on its side and, with a serrated knife, cut it into 6 layers. Mix the sour cream with the chocolate bits and coffee which have been combined in the blender at low speed. Arrange the first layer in the center of a serving plate. Spoon some of the sour cream-chocolate mixture on the layer and spread until covered. Repeat until all the layers are stacked. Spread the remaining sauce over the top and sides of the cake. Cover and chill until serving time. This cake keeps very well in the refrigerator, and improves with standing. Serves 6.

NOTE: If you don't want to bother with the blender, you can substitute ¼ cup chocolate syrup in which you have dissolved 1 tablespoon instant coffee. This method needs sweetening—use ⅓ cup confectioners' sugar.

LEMON SOUFFLE

1 package lemon
  gelatin
1 cup boiling water
1 package (8 ounces)
  cream cheese,
  softened

1 cup heavy cream,
  whipped
1 can (8 ounces)
  crushed pineapple,
  drained
½ cup coarsely
  chopped walnuts

Dissolve gelatin in boiling water. Chill until syrupy. Beat softened cream cheese into gelatin. Fold in whipped heavy cream, drained crushed pineapple, and walnuts. Turn into soufflé dish, cover with plastic wrap and chill until firm. Serves 8.

STRAWBERRIES ROMANOFF

2 pints strawberries
1 tablespoon sugar
2 tablespoons
  curaçao
½ cup heavy cream,
  whipped

½ pint vanilla
  ice cream,
  softened
2 tablespoons orange
  juice

Wash, hull, and halve strawberries. Sprinkle with sugar and curaçao (brandy or Kirsch may be substituted) and chill. At serving time, spoon berries into chilled glass bowls. Fold softened ice cream and orange juice into whipped cream. Spoon over berries. Serves 4-6.

STRAWBERRY TORTE

1¼ cups vanilla wafer   1½ pints strawberries
     crumbs*   1 jar (12 ounces)
¼ cup (½ stick)   red currant jelly
     butter, softened   ⎰ 1 cup heavy cream,
2 tablespoons sugar   ⎱   whipped, *or*
                                 ⎰ 1 cup sour cream

Combine crumbs, butter, and sugar; press
into bottom and sides of 9-inch pie tin. Chill.
Wash, hull, and slice strawberries into the
crumb crust, reserving a few whole berries for
a garnish. Stand the jar of currant jelly in a
pan of boiling water; beat with a fork until
soft. Spoon softened jelly over berries. Chill
until firm. Just before serving, top with
whipped cream or sour cream. Garnish with
whole berries. Serves 6.

*To make the crumbs, put 5 or 6 vanilla wafers into
a plastic bag; roll or pound with a heavy can. Repeat this process until you have enough crumbs for
the crust.

FROZEN DESSERTS

CRUNCHY ICE CREAM

*The flavor and texture of this variation on
ice cream are most unusual, and I recommend
it. One reservation, however. Make only as
much as you will use—it doesn't keep.*

1 tablespoon butter   flakes
¼ cup cocoa   1 pint vanilla ice
1 cup (1 ounce   cream, softened
     package) corn

In a small saucepan over low heat, melt the butter. Add the cocoa and blend until smooth. Add the corn flakes (don't crush them) and coat with the chocolate mixture. Combine quickly with softened ice cream and freeze until firm. You can do this in an ice cube tray without the dividers, in a bombe mold, or simply by packing the mixture back in the ice cream carton. Serves 4.

CHERRIES JUBILEE

1 can (1 pound) pitted black cherries	2-4 tablespoons brandy
	1½ pints vanilla ice cream

Drain about half of the cherry juice. Turn the cherries and the remaining juice into a saucepan or chafing dish. Heat until bubbling. Add brandy to taste—but remember that some of the flavor will evaporate when you ignite the cherries. Have 6 dessert glasses ready with a generous scoop of ice cream in each. Light the cherries with a match, or tip the pan sideways over the heat until it ignites with a bright blue flame. Spoon the flaming cherries (with some juice) over the ice cream. Serves 6.

FROZEN COCOANUT CREAM

1 pint vanilla ice cream	2 tablespoons crème de cacao
¼ cup flaked cocoanut	

Let ice cream soften slightly. Stir in the cocoanut and crème de cacao. Freeze. Serve with curls of shaved semisweet chocolate. Serves 4.

COFFEE CRUNCH

1 pint coffee ice cream	1 (1¾ ounces) chocolate-nut-caramel candy bar

Let ice cream soften. Slice the candy bar with a knife, and then crumble. Stir into ice cream until blended. Freeze until serving time. Serves 4.

NOTE: You can try this with many kinds of ice cream and varieties of candy. Mix vanilla ice cream with a chopped chocolate-marshmallow bar, or chocolate ice cream with a chopped peanut bar.

FROZEN COFFEE SURPRISE

1 pint coffee ice cream	3 tablespoons rum
1 teaspoon instant coffee powder	¼ cup heavy cream, whipped

Let ice cream soften slightly. Dissolve the instant coffee powder in the rum. Beat into the softened ice cream along with the whipped cream. Freeze until serving time. Serve alone or on meringues, cake shells, or ladyfingers. Serves 4.

FROZEN FRUIT PIE

1¼ cups vanilla
    wafer crumbs
¼ cup (½ stick)
    butter, softened
2 tablespoons sugar
1½ pints vanilla or
    strawberry ice
    cream

½ cup sliced fruit
    (bananas or
    strawberries)
1 cup heavy cream
½ teaspoon almond
    flavoring

Mix crumbs with butter and sugar. Spread evenly around the bottom and sides of a 9-inch pie tin. Chill the crust and let the ice cream soften. Fill the chilled crust with ice cream and arrange fruit over the top. Cover with plastic wrap and freeze until serving time. Whip heavy cream, add almond flavoring, and spread over the pie just before serving. Serves 6.

ICE CREAM WITH PLUM SAUCE

1 can (8 ounces)
    purple plums
1 tablespoon sherry
1 small stick
    cinnamon or
⅛ teaspoon
    cinnamon

1 teaspoon grated
    lemon rind or
⅛ teaspoon prepared
    lemon peel
1 pint vanilla ice
    cream
¼ cup shaved
    blanched almonds

Turn the plums with their liquid into a small bowl. Cut each plum in half and discard the pits. Add sherry. Add cinnamon and lemon. Cover and chill until serving time. Divide the ice cream into dessert bowls. Arrange 2 plum halves on each serving of ice cream and spoon some liquid over the ice cream and plums. Sprinkle shaved almonds over the top. Serves 4.

PEACH MELBA

1 can (1 pound) Elberta peach halves	½ cup heavy cream, whipped
2 tablespoons brandy, if desired	1 tablespoon confectioners' sugar
1½ pints vanilla ice cream	½ teaspoon almond flavoring
¼ cup melba sauce	¼ cup slivered almonds

If you want the brandy flavor in your peaches, turn the peaches into a large screw-top jar with part of the juice from the can and the brandy. Chill for several hours. If you don't want the brandy flavor, just chill the peaches in the can. At serving time, place a peach half with a spoon of juice in each of 6 dessert bowls. Place a generous scoop of ice cream on each peach. Drizzle the melba sauce over and around the ice cream. Flavor the whipped cream with sugar and almond, and add a generous spoonful to each dish. Top with slivered almonds. Serves 6.

FROZEN PEANUT BALL

This was the special dessert at the Drury Lane Restaurant in New York which was an old favorite. I had an editorial job in the neighborhood, and every payday I would splurge on lunch.

½ cup chocolate fudge sauce
1 pint vanilla ice cream

½ cup chopped salted peanuts

Spoon 2 tablespoons chocolate fudge sauce (hot or cold) on each dessert plate. Scoop out a ball of ice cream and roll in chopped peanuts until coated. Place carefully on sauce. Repeat for each serving. Serves 4.

NOTE: This delicious dessert lends itself to many variations. Try butterscotch sauce, coffee ice cream, and chopped almonds; or roll the ice cream in grated cocoanut and serve it with chocolate mint sauce.

INSTANT TORTONI

1 pint vanilla ice cream, softened

½ cup macaroon crumbs

While ice cream softens, make macaroon crumbs in the blender. Stir together until blended, reserving 1 tablespoon of crumbs for a garnish. Fill paper cups with the ice cream mixture, top with a sprinkling of crumbs, and freeze. Serves 4.

DESSERT SAUCES

PIQUANT GINGER SAUCE

1 cup ginger marmalade	¼ cup orange juice

Combine the ginger marmalade and orange juice in a small bowl and mix until smooth. Serve on vanilla ice cream, custard, or pudding. Makes 1 cup.

APRICOT SAUCE

1 can (1 pound) apricots	1-2 tablespoons brandy

Drain apricots; remove pits. Turn into blender. Blend at low speed to purée. Add brandy and chill. Makes 1 cup.

NOTE: Serve with ice cream, sherbet, sliced fruit, custard, or rice pudding.

CURRANT JELLY SAUCE

1 cup (9-ounce jar) currant jelly	1-2 tablespoons cognac

Beat jelly with a fork until it becomes somewhat liquid. Add cognac to taste. Serve with ice cream, custard, or sponge cake with whipped cream. Makes 1 cup.

QUICK MOCHA SAUCE

1 package (6 ounces) milk chocolate bits

¼ cup hot coffee
1 tablespoon brandy

Turn chocolate bits, hot coffee, and brandy into blender. Blend at low speed for 30 seconds. Makes 1 cup.

NOTE: Serve over vanilla, coffee, or butter pecan ice cream. Or spoon over angel, sponge, or pound cake with whipped cream and slivered almonds.

SOUR CREAM SAUCE

1 cup sour cream
⅓ cup confectioners' sugar

1 teaspoon vanilla

Stir the sour cream with confectioners' sugar and vanilla until smooth and blended. Makes 1 cup.

NOTE: Serve this sauce with hot or cold fruit, fruit pie or raisin cake.

STRAWBERRY SAUCE

1 package (10   strawberries
  ounces) frozen   1-2 tablespoons
  sweetened   Kirsch

Let the strawberries partially thaw. Turn
into the blender. Blend at low speed to purée.
Add Kirsch and chill. Makes 1 cup.
NOTE: Serve with ice cream, sherbet, sliced
fruit, custard or rice pudding, pound cake or
ladyfingers.
NOTE: This sauce can be made with frozen
sweetened raspberries.

Irresistible
Footnotes

Since the following recipes aren't numerous enough to deserve chapters of their own, I include them here as minor but mouth-watering addenda to this collection.

ONE MIRACLE CAKE AND TWO COOKIES

Quick cooking precludes baking from scratch. With so many marvelous baked products to choose from—packaged cakes and cakes shells, layer cakes, pies, and cookies—there is really no need. And there are the cake mixes which give you the feeling that you are baking without any of the bother.

But for those with the irresistible impulse to bake a cake, here is a magic recipe. It's the easiest one known, and it's really foolproof. With it are four variations that run the gamut from chocolate to apple.

There are also two uncooked cooky recipes. I've included them because they're easy and taste so good, and because they are the kind of cookies your children can make without help.

MAGIC CAKE

1 cup self-rising cake flour	2 eggs
1 cup granulated sugar	Heavy cream
	1 teaspoon vanilla

Measure 1 cup of unsifted flour; turn into medium mixing bowl. Fill same cup with sugar and add to flour. Break 2 eggs into the cup and fill it with heavy cream. Add vanilla and gradually pour into flour mixture. Stir just until blended. Pour batter into buttered 8 x 8 x 2 baking pan. Bake at 350 degrees for 40 minutes. Remove from oven and invert pan on wire rack immediately. Cool before cutting.

APPLE CREAM CAKE

2 baking apples	1 cup granulated sugar
1 tablespoon granulated sugar	2 eggs
1 teaspoon cinnamon	Heavy cream
1 cup self-rising cake flour	1 teaspoon vanilla

Core and pare apples. Cut each apple into eighths and use to line the bottom of a buttered 8 x 8 x 2 baking pan. Mix 1 tablespoon sugar with cinnamon and sprinkle over the apples. Measure the unsifted flour and empty into medium mixing bowl. Fill same cup with sugar and add. Break 2 eggs into cup and fill the cup with heavy cream. Pour into flour mixture with vanilla and stir just until blended. Cover apples with batter. Bake at 350 degrees for 40 minutes. Remove from oven and invert pan on wire rack immediately. Cool before cutting. Serve with whipped heavy cream.

COCOANUT CARAMEL CAKE

⅓ cup butter
½ cup granulated
  brown sugar
⅔ cup shredded
  cocoanut

1 cup self-rising cake
  flour
1 cup granulated
  sugar
2 eggs
  Heavy cream

Melt butter, brown sugar and cocoanut in saucepan over low heat. Line the bottom of a buttered 8 x 8 x 2 baking pan with this mixture. Measure the unsifted flour and empty into medium mixing bowl. Fill same cup with sugar and add. Break 2 eggs into cup and fill the cup with heavy cream. Pour into flour mixture and stir just until blended. Pour batter over brown sugar mixture. Bake at 350 degrees for 40 minutes. Remove from oven and invert pan on wire rack immediately. Cool before cutting.

DELICATE CHOCOLATE CAKE

1 cup self-rising cake
  flour
1 cup granulated
  sugar

2 eggs
  Heavy cream
¼ cup unsweetened
  cocoa*

Measure 1 cup unsifted flour and empty into medium mixing bowl. Fill same cup with sugar and add. Break 2 eggs into cup and fill the cup with heavy cream. Pour into flour mixture and stir just until blended. Fold in cocoa. Pour batter into buttered 8 x 8 x 2 baking pan. Bake at 350 degrees for 40 minutes. Remove from oven and invert pan on wire rack immediately. Cool before cutting. Serve topped with ice cream and Quick Mocha Sauce (See p. 203). Serves 8.

*¼ cup shaved unsweetened chocolate may be substituted for the cocoa. The taste is not as delicate, but it is delicious. Sprinkle extra shaved chocolate over the top of the baked cake while it is still warm.

NUT TORTE

1 cup self-rising cake flour	apricot jam
1 cup granulated sugar	1½ cups heavy cream
2 eggs	1 teaspoon almond flavoring
	¼ cup chopped nuts

Measure 1 cup of unsifted flour and empty into medium mixing bowl. Fill same cup with sugar and add to flour. Break 2 eggs into cup and fill the cup with heavy cream. Pour into flour mixture with almond flavoring and stir just until blended. Fold in chopped nuts. Pour batter into 2 buttered 8-inch layer pans. Bake in a 350 degree oven for 30 minutes. Remove from oven and invert pans on wire rack immediately. Cool, and then spread one layer with apricot jam, cover with second layer, and frost with flavored whipped heavy cream.

BOURBON BALLS

2 cups (1 box)   ½ cup confectioners'
  vanilla wafers,   sugar
  ground or crushed   ¼ cup chocolate
½ cup ground nuts   syrup
  (pecans, walnuts,   1-2 tablespoons
  or almonds)   bourbon

In a medium bowl, mix the ground (or crushed) wafers with nuts, sugar, chocolate syrup, and bourbon. Working quickly, pinch off enough to make a small ball, roll it between your palms, and coat with additional confectioners' sugar. If the dough gets too dry, add a drop more chocolate syrup or bourbon. This recipe makes about 2½ dozen balls, which will keep well if stored in a tin with a tight-fitting cover.

RUM BALLS

2 bars (4 ounces   3 egg whites,
  each) German   slightly beaten
  sweet chocolate   2 tablespoons rum
1 can (8 ounces)   ¼ cup shredded
  shelled walnuts   cocoanut
¾ cup sugar

Grate the chocolate in the blender at high speed. Grind the nuts with a Mouli grater into a medium bowl. Measure ¼ cup of the ground nuts and put it aside. Combine the grated chocolate and the sugar with the ground nuts. Add about ⅔ of the egg-white mixture and the rum. Shape into balls about the size of golf balls. Roll each ball in the remaining egg white and then in ground nuts or cocoanut. Set the balls into a shallow tin box with a tight-fitting cover. Leave the box open until the balls dry, then cover and store. These should keep for a week, but they'll be gone long before that! Makes about 2 dozen balls.

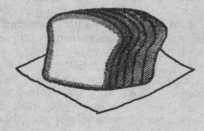

INSTANT BREADS

Here are five quick recipes for turning plebeian bread into party fare. The Cinnamon Toast recipe was worked out by my daughter, who tasted it at a college tea. It's the famous but secret recipe of the college President's wife, but undaunted, we figured it out. The trick is the thick layer of brown sugar, which gives the toast a crusty glaze. It's marvelous with coffee or tea, and a perfect dessert.

The two loaf bread recipes are a change of pace from the ubiquitous garlic bread. The hors d'oeuvres bread was born out of desperation. I wanted to serve Hummus one night, and I didn't have time to buy the flat Syrian bread, so I experimented with a tube of buttermilk biscuits. The result was creditable enough to use again and again.

The Marvelous Melba Toast is just that. It's a great recipe for slightly stale bread, and it tastes better than any packaged toast or cracker I have ever tried.

CINNAMON TOAST

8 slices white bread
½ cup butter (¼ pound) softened
2 teaspoons cinnamon
2 teaspoons sugar
1 cup granulated brown sugar

Cut crusts from bread. Toast until golden; spread with butter. Mix cinnamon with sugar and granulated brown sugar; pile on buttered toast. Toast under the broiler or in the toaster oven until glazed. Makes 8 slices.

NOTE: For each additional slice, you'll need 1 tablespoon butter, ¼ teaspoon cinnamon, ¼ teaspoon sugar, and 2 tablespoons granulated brown sugar.

TOASTED HERB LOAF

½ cup (¼ pound) butter, softened
¼ teaspoon salt
1 clove garlic, minced
¼ teaspoon dry mustard
¼ teaspoon sweet paprika
¼ teaspoon dried savory
¼ teaspoon dried thyme
1 loaf French bread

Let butter stand until very soft. Add salt, garlic, mustard, paprika, savory, and thyme and mix well. Cut bread crosswise at 2-inch intervals, but do not cut completely through. Spread the butter mixture over the top and sides of the cuts. Wrap in aluminum foil, and refrigerate. About 10 minutes before serving time, heat in the aluminum foil in a hot oven. Serves 3-4 hungry people.

HORS D'OEUVRES BREAD

1 tube buttermilk biscuits	Coarse salt
Flour	Chopped parsley

Separate the biscuits. On a lightly floured surface, roll each biscuit with a floured bottle or glass as thin as possible without tearing. Sprinkle with salt (about ¼ teaspoon per biscuit) and chopped parsley. Place in a hot oven (or toaster oven) until crisp and lightly browned—about 10 minutes. Makes 10 flat cakes.

MARVELOUS MELBA TOAST

1 package (8 ounces) thin-sliced white bread	½ pound (2 sticks) butter, softened

Spread the bread liberally with butter. Arrange on a cookie sheet, cut in squares or triangles (or leave whole). Heat in a very slow (250 degree) oven until crisp, about 30 minutes. Serve with hors d'oeuvres, soup, or salad. These will stay crisp and delicious for several days in an airtight tin. Makes about 16 slices.

SESAME STICKS

1 loaf French bread	1 teaspoon Worcestershire sauce
½ cup (¼ pound) butter, softened	1-2 tablespoons sesame seeds

Cut French bread in half; then cut each half in half again. Split each section lengthwise. You should have 8 pieces. Mix butter with Worcestershire sauce. Butter all the cut surfaces with the butter mixture. About 10 minutes before serving time, arrange the sticks in a foil baking dish, sprinkle with sesame seeds and heat in a hot oven until brown and crusty. Makes 8 rolls.

SPECIAL SANDWICHES

Everybody knows that sandwiches are quick and easy, and I'm not about to belabor the obvious. Here are some that may be just different enough to add variety to your sandwich repertoire.

DJ'S CROQUE MONSIEUR

DJ's is the name of a tearoom my twin daughters ran one summer when they were sixteen. They are both great cooks, and this was the most popular dish on the menu.

8 slices thin rye bread	8 slices boiled ham
¼ cup butter, softened	8 slices Swiss cheese
1 clove garlic, crushed	

Toast the bread lightly. Spread with softened butter which has been mixed with garlic. Top each slice with a slice of ham and then a slice of cheese. Place in toaster oven or under broiler until cheese melts.

NOTE: To make Croque Madame, use slices of boiled chicken instead of boiled ham.

GRILLED GOURMET SANDWICHES

4 slices French
  bread (½ inch
  thick)
¼ cup butter,
  softened
1 tablespoon chopped
  chives
1 tablespoon
  chopped parsley

8 artichoke bottoms
  or mushroom caps
1 cup (7 ounce can)
  finely diced
  chicken
⅓ cup shredded
  Gruyère cheese

Spread the bread with butter mixed with chopped chives and parsley. Put 2 artichoke bottoms or mushroom caps on each slice. Top with chicken. Sprinkle cheese over chicken. Place in toaster oven or under broiler until cheese melts. Serves 2-3.

SANDWICH NICOISE

6 individual French
  loaves
½ cup butter,
  softened
1 can (7 ounces)
  white tuna fish,
  drained
1 can (2 ounces)
  anchovy fillets,
  drained
1 cucumber, peeled
2 tomatoes

2 hard-cooked eggs
2 tablespoons capers
1 tablespoon
  chopped parsley
6 tablespoons olive
  oil
3 tablespoons white
  wine vinegar
1 teaspoon Dijon
  mustard
6 Boston lettuce
  leaves

Cut each loaf in half. (If you can't find individual French loaves, you can use long, hard rolls.) Hollow out the bottom of each half, and spread both halves with softened butter. In a medium bowl, flake the drained tuna. In a wooden bowl, chop the drained anchovy fillets with the cucumber, tomatoes, and eggs. Add to tuna with capers and parsley. In a small screw-top jar, combine oil with vinegar and mustard. Mix with salad. Divide the salad on the 6 hollowed-out halves. Cover each with a leaf of Boston lettuce. Top each with its remaining half to make a sandwich. Serves 6.

QUICK PIZZA

4 English muffins	½ cup canned
¼ cup butter,	marinara sauce
softened	1 teaspoon oregano
1 clove garlic,	¼ pound (8 slices)
crushed	mozzarella cheese

Break apart muffins. Toast lightly. Mix softened butter with crushed garlic clove. Spread on muffins. Top each half with marinara sauce, a pinch of oregano, and a generous slice of cheese. Place in toaster oven or under broiler until cheese melts. Serves 3-4.

NOTE: You can vary the taste of Quick Pizzas by adding one of the following—anchovy fillets, sliced sweet or spicy sausage, minced clams or mushrooms.

TOMATO SURPRISE SANDWICHES

4 English muffins	2 large tomatoes
2-3 tablespoons	¼ cup mayonnaise
anchovy paste	¼ cup sour cream

Break apart muffins. Toast lightly. Spread each half with anchovy paste—use sparingly for subtle flavoring, more for a definite anchovy taste. Top each half with a generous slice of tomato. Mix mayonnaise and sour cream until smooth, then spoon over tomatoes. Place in toaster oven or under broiler until heated. Serves 3-4.

CHEESE DISHES

Cheese is a valuable food for the quick cook; it keeps in the refrigerator, and blends comfortably with other ingredients. Here are some cheese casseroles than can be thrown together in a matter of minutes, with bread and milk, to make delicious snacks or suppers. Served with crusty bread and tossed green salad, they make a meal.

With the advent of the frozen pie crust,

quiche and quiche variations come into the quick-cooking category. The quiches here are simple, easily assembled, and perfect every time. Use them for hors d'oeuvres, luncheon, or supper or even for dinner with sliced cold meat.

NOODLES WITH CHEESE

1 package (8 ounces) noodles
1 cup cottage cheese
1 package (8 ounces) cream cheese
½ cup sour cream
½ cup snipped scallions
1 teaspoon coarse salt
Freshly ground black pepper
1 clove garlic, crushed
¼ cup freshly grated Parmesan cheese

Cook noodles according to directions on package. While the noodles are cooking, mix cottage cheese, cream cheese, sour cream, scallions, salt, pepper, and crushed garlic. Drain noodles and add to cheese mixture. Turn into a buttered 2-quart casserole. Heat in a moderately hot (375 degree) oven for 20 minutes. Sprinkle with Parmesan cheese and heat for 10 minutes more—30 minutes in all. Serves 4-6.

ONION CHEESE PIE

8 slices bread
½ cup (¼ pound) butter
8 slices Muenster, American, or cheddar cheese
1 cup sliced onion rings
3 eggs
1½ cups milk
1 teaspoon coarse salt
½ teaspoon Worcestershire sauce
Freshly ground black pepper

Spread the bread with ¼ cup of the butter. Arrange in a single layer in a buttered shallow baking dish. Cover each slice of buttered bread with a slice of cheese. Melt the remaining ¼ cup of butter, and sauté the onion rings until transparent. Arrange over cheese. Beat eggs slightly. Add milk, salt, Worcestershire, and pepper. Pour over onions. Bake in a moderately slow (325 degree) oven for 25 to 30 minutes or until set. Serves 4.

OYSTER RAREBIT

1 pound Swiss cheese
½ cup dry white wine
1 teaspoon Dijon mustard
½ teaspoon coarse salt
12 fresh oysters *or* 1 can (7 ounces) frozen oysters, defrosted

Cut the cheese into small cubes in a fondue pot or medium skillet over low heat. Add wine, mustard, and salt. Stir over low heat until cheese begins to melt. Add the fresh or defrosted oysters which have been carefully drained and cook for 2 to 3 minutes more. Serve with French bread or toast. Serves 4-5.

SUNDAY CHEESE BAKE

6 slices white bread	2 eggs
3 tablespoons butter, softened	1 cup milk
½ clove garlic, crushed	¾ teaspoon coarse salt
1 cup grated sharp cheddar cheese	¼ teaspoon paprika
	¼ teaspoon dry mustard

Trim the crusts off the bread. Mix butter with crushed garlic. Butter the bread, and cut each slice into 4 squares. Line the bottom of a buttered oven-proof casserole with bread squares. Sprinkle with grated cheese. Alternate bread and cheese again. Beat eggs lightly. Add milk and seasonings; beat just until combined. Pour over the bread and cheese. Heat in a moderate oven until firm—about 30 minutes. Serves 3 hungry people or 4 with normal appetites.

SWISS TOAST

6 slices white bread	1 cup cream or milk
¼ cup white wine	1 teaspoon grated
1½ cups grated Swiss	onion
cheese	½ teaspoon coarse
¼ cup sliced	salt
mushrooms (or	½ teaspoon dry
ripe olives)	mustard
2 eggs, slightly	Freshly ground
beaten	black pepper

Cut the bread into cubes. Arrange the cubes in a buttered oven-proof casserole. Pour white wine over the bread cubes, and let stand while you prepare the rest of the dish. Mix 1 cup of the grated Swiss cheese and the mushrooms or olives with the soaked bread cubes. In a small bowl, beat the eggs slightly. Add cream or milk, onion, salt, mustard, and pepper. Pour over the cheese mixture. Sprinkle the remaining ½ cup of the cheese over the top. Bake in a very hot oven (450 degrees) for 15 to 20 minutes or until puffed and brown. Serves 2-3 hungry people or 4 people as a late-night snack.

KAREN'S QUICHE

3 eggs	shredded Swiss
1 cup sour cream	cheese
¾ teaspoon salt	1 can (3½ ounces)
½ teaspoon	French fried
Worcestershire	onion rings
sauce	9-inch pastry shell,
1 cup coarsely	baked and cooled

Beat eggs slightly. Add sour cream, salt, Worcestershire sauce, Swiss cheese, and French fried onions. Pour into baked, cooled shell. Heat in a slow (300 degree) oven for 30 minutes or until set. Place under broiler for 1-2 minutes before serving. Serves 6.

QUICK QUICHE

8-inch frozen pastry shell, thawed
1 cup diced cooked ham
1¼ cups grated Gruyère cheese

2 eggs, slightly beaten
1 cup light or heavy cream
¾ teaspoon coarse salt
Freshly ground black pepper

Sprinkle the ham and 1 cup of the cheese into the thawed pastry shell. In a small bowl combine the slightly beaten eggs, the cream, salt, and pepper. Pour over ham and cheese mixture. Sprinkle the remaining ¼ cup of cheese over the top. Bake in a hot oven (400 degrees) for 35-45 minutes, or until pastry is brown and filling is set. Serves 4-6.

NOTE: This quiche can be made with cheddar or Swiss cheese.

QUICK QUICHE PROVENCAL

8-inch frozen pastry shell, thawed	½ cup sliced pitted ripe olives
¾ cup freshly grated Parmesan cheese	2 eggs, slightly beaten
½ cup thinly sliced scallions	¾ cup heavy cream
1 large tomato, peeled*	½ teaspoon coarse salt
1 tablespoon flour	Freshly ground black pepper

Sprinkle about ¼ cup of the cheese into the bottom of the pastry shell. Sprinkle half of the scallions over the cheese. Slice the tomato. Dust the slices with flour, then arrange in one layer. Sprinkle with another ¼ cup of cheese, scallions, and sliced olives. Mix slightly beaten eggs with cream. Add salt and pepper and pour over tomatoes. Sprinkle remaining cheese over the top. Bake in a hot oven (400 degrees) for 35-45 minutes or until pastry is brown and filling is set. Serves 4-6.

*To peel tomato, cover for 1 to 2 minutes with boiling water. Spear tomato at blossom end with fork and with the tip of a sharp knife, remove the skin.

RELISHES

Here are four relishes to consider. They are so easy to make that you won't believe how good they taste. The two cranberry molds are perfect for Thanksgiving dinner; the other two might be part of an antipasto tray. Try any one of them to give zest to an unexciting meal.

MOLDED CRANBERRY RELISH

1 pound raw
  cranberries
1 cup sugar
2 packages cherry or
  strawberry gelatin
1 cup boiling water
1 can (1 pound)
  crushed pineapple

Chop cranberries in blender at high speed or put through meat grinder. Add sugar and let stand for 30 minutes. Dissolve gelatin in boiling water. Add crushed pineapple with liquid and cranberry-sugar mixture. Turn into mold which has been rinsed in cold water. Chill until firm. Serves 6-8.

CRANBERRY-APPLE MOLD

1 package cherry or
  strawberry gelatin
1 cup boiling water
1 can (1 pound)
  whole cranberry
  sauce
1 cup applesauce
½ teaspoon grated
  lemon rind

Dissolve gelatin in boiling water, Add cranberry sauce, applesauce, and lemon rind. Turn into mold which has been rinsed in cold water. Chill until firm. Serves 4-6.

PICKLED CAULIFLOWER

1 cup liquid from a   1 cup cauliflowerets
 jar of spicy pickles

Save the pickling liquid from any kind of kosher, dill, or sweet pickles. Add the cut-up cauliflower and marinate in the refrigerator for several days. Serve as a relish.

NOTE: You can do the same thing with carrot sticks, mushrooms, young brussel sprouts, and whole string beans.

GARLIC OLIVES WITH NUTS

1 can (7½ ounces)   1 cup liquid from
 pitted extra large   kosher or spicy
 black olives   pickles
1 package (4 ounces)   5 or 6 cloves of garlic
 shelled whole
 almonds

Drain olives. Stuff an almond into each olive; don't put it in far enough to split the olive—the top quarter of each almond should be visible. Put the stuffed olives into a large screw-top jar. Add the pickling liquid and the cut garlic cloves. Chill for 24 hours.

INDEX

Aioli sauce, 145
Anchovies
  artichoke salad, 118
  butter sauce, 11, 142
  cream dressing, 134-135
  dips, 27, 30-31
  guacamole, 38
  Marge's Liptauer, 30-31
  peppers and, 31
  remoulade sauce, 148
  salad dressings, 118-119, 134-135
Antipasto, 31-42
Appetizers, 25, 31-42
  anchovies and peppers, 31-32
  cannellini with caviar, 33
  cheese ball I and II, 35
  crabmeat turnovers, 36
  Esther's pâté I and II, 36-38
  frankfurters, 98
  guacamole, 38
  herring with apples, 39
  marinated mushrooms, 34
  melon with prociutto, 39
  Nicky's pâté, 41-42
  pickled olives, 34
  roast beef rolls, 98
  salmon mousse, 66-67
  scallop seviche, 39-40
  shrimp in mustard sauce, 40-41
  shrimp Toledo, 41
  spiced beans, 32
Apples
  Charlotte, 186
  cranberry mold, 226
  cream cake, 208-209
  graham pudding, 190
  herring and, 39
  red cabbage and, 158
  Waldorf salad, 134
Appliances, 9, 14
Apricots
  Bavarian cream, 186-187
  sauce, 202
Artichokes
  and anchovy salad, 118
  chicken with, 77 78
  with rice, 174
Asparagus with lemon butter sauce, 154
Avgolemono sauce, 142
Avocados
  chicken salad in, 123
  and clam bisque, 46
  guacamole, 38
  salad, 118-119
  sauce, 145
  shrimp bisque, 55
  spicy dip, 27-28

Baked beans, 154-155
Bananas, glazed, 187
Beans
  baked, 154-155
  black, dips, 28
  cannellini (white kidney)

quick cassoulet, 99-
    100
with caviar, 33
chick peas
    spiced, 32
Wendy's Hummus, 30
green
    casserole, 155
    melange, 155-156
    with mushrooms, 156
    salad, 119-120
lima
    au gratin, 156
    bean slaw, 121
    frankfurter casserole,
        97
    soup, 52
    with water chestnuts,
        157
Patty's bean salad I
    and II, 119-120
red kidney, 175
slaw, 121
Béarnaise sauce, 144
Beef
    baked hamburgers, 88-
        89
    fondue Bourguignonne,
        111-112
    grilled flank steak, 109-
        110
    Pattie's casserole, 93-
        94
    roast beef rolls, 98
    speedy meat loaf, 89
    steak Tartare, 89-90
    Stroganoff, 88
    tongue and ham with
        mushrooms, 95
Beets, quick borscht, 46
Black bean dip, 28
Borscht, quick, 46
Bourbon balls, 211
Bread and rolls, 212-215
    cinnamon toast, 213
    garlic, 11
    for hors d'oeuvres, 214
    melba toast, 214-215

plastic bags for, 11
sandwiches, 216-219
sesame sticks, 215
toasted herb loaf, 213-
    214
Butters
    anchovy, 11, 142
    composed, 11
    garlic, 11, 143
    herb, 11, 143
    sauces, 142-143
        anchovy, 142
        chive, 143
        curry, 143
        garlic, 143
        herb, 143
        lemon, 154
        mustard, 143
        scallion, 178
        tarragon, 143

Cabbage
    bean slaw, 121
    Chinese, 158
    cole slaw, 126
    red cabbage with ap-
        ple, 158
    Savoy salad, 121-122
    soup, 47
Cakes
    apple cream, 208-209
    cocoanut caramel, 209
    delicate chocolate, 209-
        210
    magic, 208
    nut torte, 210
    orange cream, 192
    seven layer surprise,
        194
    surprise, 193-194
Can sizes, 19
Cannellini (white kidney
    beans)
    with caviar, 33
    quick cassoulet, 99-100
Carrots
    cream of carrot soup,
        47

with grapes, 159
Tsimmis, 159
Casseroles, 12
  asparagus-chicken, 76
  baked chicken with
    ham, 77
  frankfurters, 97
  green bean, 155
  quick cassoulet, 99-100
  seafood, 179
  Sunday cheese bake,
    222
  Swiss toast, 223
  tuna fish, 71-72
  turkey, 82-83
Cauliflower
  au gratin, 160
  pickled, 227
  surprise salad, 122
Caviar, 25
  cannelini with, 33
  consomme madrilene,
    48
  dip, 29
  sauce, 145
Chafing dish cookery
  David's rabbit, 112-113
  Monterey Jack, 113
Cheese, 219-225
  cheese ball I and II,
    35
  cream cheese; see
    Cream cheese
  David's rabbit, 112-113
  dips, 28-31
  Karen's quiche, 223-
    224
  Monterey Jack, 113
  noodles and, 220
  and onion pie, 221
  oyster rarebit, 221-222
  Parmesan, 10
  quiches, 223-225
  Roquefort dip, 29
  Roquefort dressings I
    and II, 136-137, 146
  and shrimp bake, 68-69
  storing, 10

Sunday cheese bake,
  222
Swiss toast, 223
Chef salad, 123
Cherries
  chicken with, 79
  jubilee, 197
Chick peas
  spiced beans, 32
  Wendy's Hummus, 30
Chicken
  with artichokes, 77-78
  and asparagus casse-
    role, 76
  baked with ham, 77
  breasts with tarragon,
    79-80
  cacciatore, 78
  chef salad, 123
  with cherries, 79
  condensed broth, 10
  grilled Polynesian, 109
  honey-glazed, 76-77
  livers sauté, 84
  oven-fried I and II, 80-
    81
  salad, 123-124
  sandwiches, 216-217
  Véronique, 81-82
Chinese cabbage, 158
Chives
  butter sauce, 143
  green cheese dip, 28-29
Chocolate
  cake, 209-210
  mocha sauce, 203
  mousse, 191
  seven layer cake, 194
  wafer roll, 187-188
Chutney sauce, 146
Cinnamon toast, 213
Clams
  and avocado bisque, 46
  baked, 60
  hors d'oeuvres, 25
  puree mongole with,
    54

sauce, 181
Cocoanut
    caramel cake, 209
    frozen cream, 197-198
Coffee
    frozen surprise, 198
    ice cream crunch, 198
    toffee tart, 188
Comsommé Russe, 48
Conversion table for
    equivalents, 20-21
Cookies
    bourbon balls, 211
    crumbs, 11
    rum balls, 211-212
Cookware, 11-12
    disposable, 11-12
Corn
    colorful, 161
    grilled, 107
Crabmeat
    au gratin, 61-62
    baked, 60-61
    bisque, 49
    hot salad, 62
    salad, 124-125
    turnovers, 36
Cranberries
    and apple mold, 226
    frankfurters and, 98
    molded relish, 225-226
Cream cheese
    dips, 28-31
        green cheese, 28-29
        Marge's Liptauer,
            30-31
        spicy avocado, 27-28
    guacamole, 38
Croque Madame, 216
Croque Monsieur, 216
Crudités (raw vegeta-
    bles), 26-27
Crumbs, cookie and
    cracker, 11, 61
Cucumbers
    cheese dip, 28-29
    frosty soup, 49

salad, 126
in sour cream, 127
Currant jelly sauce, 202-
    203
Curry
    butter sauce, 143
    cold rice with, 175-176
    iced soup, 50
    shrimp, 69

David's rabbit, 112-113
David's shallot sauce,
    148
Deep-fat frying, 17
Desserts, 185-204
    apple Charlotte, 186
    apricot Bavarian
        cream, 186-187
    cakes; see Cakes
    chocolate mousse, 191
    chocolate wafer roll,
        187-188
    coffee toffee tart, 188
    frozen, 196-202; see
        also Frozen desserts
    fruit Bavarian cream,
        189
    gelatin, 12; see also
        Gelatin desserts
    gingered figs, 189
    graham apple pudding,
        190
    grape surprise, 190
    lemon soufflé, 195
    lemon syllabub, 191-
        192
    nut torte, 210
    orange cream cake,
        192
    orange sherbet mold,
        193
    rice pudding, 177-178
    sauces, 202-204
        apricot, 202
        currant jelly, 202-
            203
        mocha, 203
        piquant ginger, 202

sour cream, 203
strawberry, 204
seven layer surprise cake, 194
strawberries Romanoff, 195
strawberry torte, 196
surprise cake, 193-194
Dill sauce, 146
Dips, 25, 26-31
anchovy, 27
black bean, 28
crudités (raw vegetables), 26-27
green cheese, 28-29
Marge's Liptauer, 30-31
quick dip, 29
red caviar, 29
spicy avocado, 27-28
Wendy's Hummus, 30
Duckling in orange sauce, 83

Eggplant appetizers, 33-34
Eggs
avgolemono sauce, 142
Hollandaise sauce, 143
Endive, braised, 157
Esther's pâté I and II, 36-37
Equivalents, conversion table for, 20-21

Figs, gingered, 189
Fish and shellfish
broiling, 59
clams, 25, 54
baked, 60
sauce, 181
crabmeat
au gratin, 61-62
baked, 60-61
hot salad, 62
salad, 124-125
escabeche of flounder, 64-65

fillets
in cream sauce, 63
oven-fried, 64
in shrimp sauce, 63
frozen, 59
haddock, broiled, 59
lobster, molded ring, 65
oysters Lafitte, 66
oysters rarebit, 221-222
salads
Nicoise, 130-131
smoked fish, 132
salmon
mousse, 66-67
in shells, 67-68
scallops
broiled with wine, 68
seviche, 39-40
seafood casserole, 179
shrimp
and cheese bake, 68-69
cold curried rice, 175
curry, 69
and rice, 70
seviche, 70
striped bass, broiled, 59
swordfish
broiled, 59
grilled, 110-111
tuna fish
casserole, 71-72
salad Nicoise, 130-131
sandwich Nicoise, 217
sauces, 150
Fondue, 111
Bourguignonne, 111-112
Frankfurters
easy choucroute, 95-96
lima bean casserole, 97
sweet and sour, 98

French dressings
  basic, 135
  sour cream, 136
Frozen desserts, 196-202
  cherries jubilee, 197
  cocoanut cream, 197-
    198
  coffee crunch, 198
  coffee surprise, 198
  crunchy ice cream, 196
  fruit pie, 199
  ice cream with plum
    sauce, 199-200
  instant tortoni, 201-202
  peach melba, 200
  peanut ball, 201
Fruit
  Bavarian cream, 189
  frozen fruit pie, 199
  glazed bananas, 187
  melon with prosciutto,
    39
  peach melba, 200
  salad
    lime cream mold,
      128-129
    mold, 129-130
    Philip's tropical, 131
    Waldorf salad, 134

Garlic
  Aioli sauce, 145
  bread, 11
  butter, 11, 143
  olives with nuts, 227
  toasted herb bread,
    213-214
Gazpacho I and II, 50-51
Gelatin desserts
  apricot Bavarian
    cream, 186-187
  chocolate mousse, 191
  fruit Bavarian cream,
    189
  lemon souffle, 195
  orange sherbet mold,
    193

Ginger
  figs, 189
  piquant sauce, 202
Grapes
  carrots with, 159
  surprise dessert, 190
Gravies, use of canned,
    10
Green beans
  casserole, 155
  mélange, 155-156
  with mushrooms, 156
  Patty's salad I and II,
    119-120
Ground Floor salad, 127-
    128
Guacamole, 26, 38

Haddock, broiled, 59
Ham
  chef salad, 123
  chicken baked with, 77
  with currant glaze, 94
  Hoppin' John, 176
  orange-glazed, 94
  prosciutto with melon,
    39
  quiche, 223-225
  salad, 129
  sandwiches, 216
  and tongue with mush-
    rooms, 95
Hamburgers, 88-89
  grilled, 106
Herbs, 12-13
  butter sauce, 143
  dried, 13
  growing fresh, 12-13
  storing, 12-13
  toasted herb bread, 213
Herring with apples, 39
Hollandaise sauce, 143-
    144
Hoppin' John, 176
Hors d'oeuvres, 25-42
  appetizers, 31-42; see
    also Appetizers
  bread for, 214

dips, 25, 26-31; *see also* Dips
Horseradish
  mayonnaise sauce, 146
  with sour cream, 149
Hummus, 26, 30
  Wendy's, 30

Ice cream
  cherries jubilee, 197
  coffee crunch, 198
  crunchy, 196-197
  frozen cocoanut cream, 197-198
  frozen coffee surprise, 198
  frozen fruit pie, 199
  frozen peanut ball, 201
  instant Tortoni, 201-202
  peach Melba, 200
  with plum sauce, 199

Knockwurst
  easy choucroute, 95-96
  and sauerkraut, 97

Lamb
  broiled chops, 90-91
  grilled (leg) butterfly, 108
Lemon
  butter sauce, 154
  juice, use of, 10
  soufflé, 195
  syllabub, 191-192
Lima beans
  au gratin, 156
  frankfurter casserole, 97
  soup, 52
  with water chestnuts, 157
Lime
  cream salad mold, 128-129
  escabeche of flounder, 64-65

scallops marinated in, 39-40
shrimp seviche, 70
Liverwurst pâté I and II, 36-38
Lobster ring, 65

Marge's Liptauer (dip), 30-31
Mayonnaise
  blender, 145
  sauces, 145-147
    Aioli (garlic), 145
    avocado, 145
    caviar, 146
    chutney, 146
    dill, 146
    horseradish, 146
    mayonnaise verte, 147
    mint, 146
    orange, 146
    remoulade, 148
    Roquefort, 146
    Russian dressing, 146
    Tartar sauce, 146
Measurements, 15-16
  abbreviations, 15
Meat
  barbecued spareribs, 107
  beef
    baked hamburgers, 88-89
    fondue Bourguignonne, 111
    grilled flank steak, 109-110
    grilled steak Roquefort, 110
    hamburgers, grilled, 106
    meatballs, 98
    Patti's casserole, 93
    quick cassoulet, 99-100
    roast beef rolls, 98

second-day steak, 99
speedy meat loaf, 89
steak Tartare, 89-90
Stroganoff, 88
tongue and ham, 95
calf's liver with sour
cream, 101
canned meats, 87
charcoal cooking, 105-
113
frankfurters; see Frank-
furters
ham
easy choucroute, 95-
96
orange-glazed, 94
and tongue, 95
knockwurst
easy choucroute, 95-
96
and sauerkraut, 97
lamb
broiled chops, 90-91
grilled (leg), 108
sausage
easy choucroute, 95-
96
quick cassoulet, 99
temperatures for cook-
ing, 18-19
veal
with black olives, 92
braised chops, 92-93
with lemon, 91
Melba toast, 214-215
Melon with prosciutto, 39
Mint mayonnaise, 146
Mocha sauce, 203
Monterey Jack, 113
Mushrooms
green beans with, 156
marinated, 11, 34
tongue and ham with,
95
Mustard
butter sauce, 143
shrimp in, 40-41

Nicky's pâté, 41-42
Noodles with cheese,
220
Nuts, 10
torte, 210

Okra, southern, 161
Olives
pickled, 11, 34
stuffed with almonds,
227
Onions
cheese pie, 221
frozen chopped, 10
with nuts, 162
soup, 32-53
Oranges
cream cake, 192
duckling in orange
sauce, 83
mayonnaise sauce, 146
sherbet mold, 193
shrimp Toledo, 41
Oysters
Lafitte, 66
rarebit, 221

Pâtés
Esther's pâté I and II,
36-38
Nicky's Pâté, 41-42
Peaches
brandy, 11
melba, 200
Peas
with dill, 163
French-style, 162-163
minted, 163
Peppers with anchovies,
31
Philip's tropical fruit
salad, 131-132
Pineapple
lime cream salad mold,
128-129
molded cranberry rel-
ish, 226
Pizza, 218

Plum sauce, 199
Potatoes
  in cream, 164
  hot potato salad, 164
  scalloped, 165
Poultry, 75
  canned roasts, 75
  chicken; see Chicken
  duckling in orange sauce, 83
  ready-cooked barbecued, 75
  turkey, 75
    and wild rice, 82-83
Pumpkin soup, 53
Puree mongole with clams, 54

Quiches, 223-225
  Karen's, 223-224
  Provencal, 225
  quick, 224

Raspberry sauce, 204
Relishes, 225-227
  cranberry-apple mold, 226
  garlic olives with nuts, 227
  molded cranberry relish, 226
  pickled cauliflower, 227
Remoulade sauce, 148
Rice, 173-181
  al pesto, 177
  with artichokes, 174
  canned, 173
  Chinese, 173
  clam sauce for, 180
  cold curried, 175
  Hoppin' John, 176
  Italian rice salad, 125
  pudding, 177
  red beans with, 175
  scallions and, 178
  seafood casserole, 179
  shrimp and, 70-71
  spinach and, 180

Trieste, 180-181
turkey and wild rice, 82-83
Roquefort dressing
  with mayonnaise, 146
  with oil and vinegar, 137
  with sour cream, 136
Rum balls, 211
Russian dressing, 146

Salads and salad dressings, 117-128
  artichoke, 118
  avocados, 118
  bean slaw, 121
  cauliflower, 122
  chef salad, 123
  chicken in avocado, 123
  cold curried rice, 175
  crab supreme, 124
  cucumbers in sour cream, 127
  Donna's chicken, 124
  dressings
    anchovy, 118
    basic French, 135
    cream, 134-135
    mayonnaise, 145-147; see also Mayonnaise
    Roquefort, 136-137, 146
    sour cream French, 136
    vinaigrette, 130
  fruit salad mold, 129
  Ground Floor salad, 127
  ham, 129
  hot crabmeat, 62
  hot potato, 164
  Italian rice, 125
  Jane's cole slaw, 126
  molded, 12
    fruit salad, 129
    lime cream, 128-129

old-fashioned cucumber, 126
Patty's bean salad I and II, 119-120
Philip's tropical fruit, 131
rice, 174
salade Niçoise, 130
Savoy cabbage, 121
smoked fish, 132
spiced chick peas, 32
spinach salad, 132
stuffed tomatoes, 133
Waldorf, 134
Salmon
  mousse, 66-67
  in shells, 67
  smoked, 25
Sandwiches, 216-219
  Croque Madame, 216
  Croque Monsieur, 216
  grilled gourmet, 217
  ham and Swiss cheese, 216
  Niçoise, 217-218
  Pizza, 218
  tomato surprise, 219
Sauces, 141-150
  avgolemono, 142
  Béarnaise, 144
  butter, 142-143
    anchovy, 142
    chive, 143
    curry, 143
    garlic, 143
    herb, 143
    lemon, 154
    mustard, 143
    scallion, 178
    tarragon, 143
  canned, 10
  clam, 181
  dessert, 202-204
    apricot, 202
    currant jelly, 202
    piquant ginger, 202
    quick mocha, 203
    raspberries, 204

sour cream, 203
strawberry, 204
  Hollandaise, 143
  mayonnaise, 145-147; see also Mayonnaise
  mustard, 40
  orange, 83
  plum, 147, 199
  remoulade, 148
  savory hot, 144
  shallot, 148
  sour cream and horseradish, 149
  tomato, 149
  tuna fish, 150
  use of canned gravies, 83
Sauerkraut
  with dill, 167
  easy choucroute, 95-96
  and knockwurst, 97
Sausage
  easy choucroute, 95-96
  quick cassoulet, 99-100
Scallops
  broiled with wine, 68
  marinated, 39
  seviche, 39-40
Seafood casserole, 179
Seasonings, 13
Sesame sticks, 215
Shellfish; see Fish and shellfish
Shrimps
  bisque, 55
  and cheese bake, 68
  cold curried rice, 175
  curry, 69
  in mustard sauce, 40
  with rice, 70
  seviche, 70
  Toledo, 41
Soups, 45-56
  borscht, 46
  chilled
    avocado-clam bisque, 46
    consommé Russe, 48

cucumber, 49
Gazpacho I and II, 50
iced curry, 50
tomato dill, 54
Vichyssoise, 56
crab bisque, 49
cream of carrot, 47
creamy pumpkin, 53
creamy vegetable, 48
lima bean, 52
Millie's cabbage, 47
onion, 52-53
puree mongole with clams, 54
ready-to-serve, 45
savory spinach, 55
serving, 45
sherry added, 45
shrimp bisque, 55
stock, 10
tomato dill, 54
Sour cream
anchovy dip, 27
cucumbers in, 127
dessert sauce, 203
French dressing, 136
herring with apples, 38
and horseradish sauce, 149
seven layer cake, 194
surprise cake, 193
Spareribs, barbecued, 107
Spiced beans, 32
Spinach
and rice, 180
salad, 132
savory, 167
soup, 55
Squash with peanuts, 168
Steak Tartare, 89
Strawberries
fruit Bavarian cream, 189
Romanoff, 195
sauce, 204
torte, 196
Sunday cheese bake, 222

Sweet potatoes
carrot Tsimmis, 159
with marshmallows, 165
supreme, 166
Swiss toast, 223
Swordfish
broiled, 59
grilled, 110

Tarragon and butter sauce, 143
Tartar sauce, 146
Temperatures, 16-19
deep-fat frying, 17
for meat, 18-19
oven, 16-17
Toasted herb loaf, 213
Tomatoes
dill soup, 54
Gazpacho I and II, 50
green bean melange, 155
grilled, 168
salad, 133-134
sauce, 149
surprise sandwiches, 219
Tortes
nut, 210
strawberry, 196
Tortoni, 201-202
Tuna fish
casserole, 71
salade Nicoise, 130
sandwich Nicoise, 217
sauces, 150
Turkey
Ground Floor salad, 127
and wild rice, 82-83

Veal
with black olives, 92
braised chops, 92-93
with lemon, 91
Vegetables, 153-169
asparagus, 154
baked beans, 154
braised endive, 157

canned, 153
carrots
  with grapes, 159
  Tsimmis, 159
cauliflower
  au gratin, 160
  pickled, 227
  surprise salad, 122
Chinese cabbage, 158
colorful corn, 161
creamy soup, 48
frozen, 153
green beans
  casserole, 153
  mélange, 155
  with mushrooms, 156
lima beans
  au gratin, 156
  frankfurters and, 97
  soup, 52

marinated, 12
okra, 161
onions with nuts, 162
peas, 162-163
potatoes, 164-165
raw (*crudités*), 26-27
red cabbage, 158
sauerkraut, 167
seasoning, 153
spinach, 167
squash with peanuts,
  168
sweet potatoes, 165-
  166
tomatoes grilled, 168
zucchini bake, 169
Vichyssoise soup, 56
Vinaigrette dressing, 130

Waldorf salad, 134